Reflections
of a
Thought

GADIER HEIN GARCIA

Raw Earth Ink

2024

First paperback edition January 2024

Edited by Candice Louisa Daquin
All photos by Gadier Hein Garcia
Book design by tara caribou

ISBN 978-1-960991-19-5 (paperback)

Published by Raw Earth Ink
PO Box 39332
Ninilchik, AK 99639
www.raw-earth-ink.com

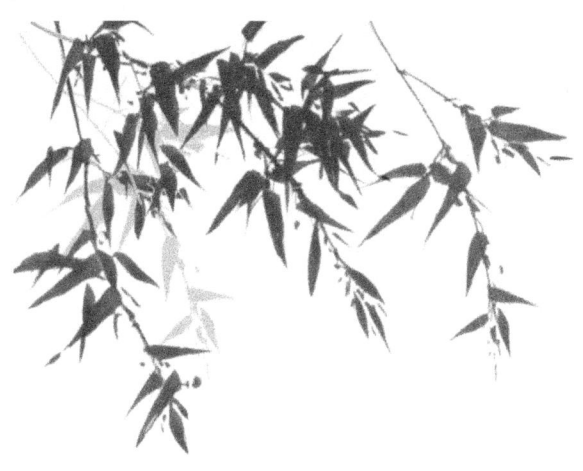

For
All my family and friends
who helped me become the person I am today.

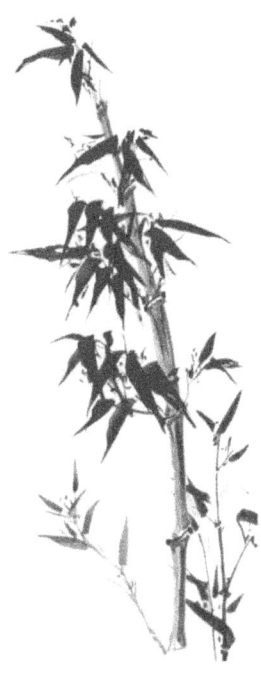

Introduction

Hello Friends, who have opened this book. This is a book of my thoughts that have come to me throughout my lifetime. My thoughts or proverbs are considerations that a person can choose to read and from this, reflect on their different meanings at different times throughout a lifetime.

When a person reads one thought on any day of their lives, they may have a curtain outlook or experience an unhelpful introspection as a result of this thought. However, if that person reads that same thought on another day, they may have another outlook or consideration of that same passage of words. In many ways, this is due to our own growth, the passing of time, gained wisdom, and varied emotional changes that a person develops with the passage of time.

This is one element of many, to consider the vast greatness of life and people. To be able to experience one simple or complex thought during a single moment and have a curtained introspective outlook or answer. Then to come back to that same simple or complex thought one hour, one day, or one year later with a totally different introspective outlook and from this, the answer being sought emerges.

What makes us change our minds and feelings towards a mere grouping of words? This is a question worth looking into individually. As all people have their own life experiences and cognitive processes, these are some of the elements that create an individual. These life experiences and cognitive processes mold a simple core in everybody, *Habitual Individuality*.

We humans are creatures of habit and tend to have a set routine in the way we perform a task and think or make it easier for the individual.

In some respects, the Eastern way of life is very different than the Western way of life. In the East there is more emphasis on an internalized process or way of life, whereas for the West it's typically more of an externalized process or way of life. Both the East and West have their positive and negative aspects, like all things in this world. In Western society, one of the main goals is to find and prove truth through rational, scientific and logical methods as taught to us in school. This is more of an externalized approach. However, in Eastern society, one of the main goals or way of life, is to accept truth and find balance by studying Buddhism, Taoism, and Zen. This is more of an internalized approach. If an individual can unearth and acquire certain skills from both the East and the West, this individual can become a more positive influence on themselves, family, and their community.

In Zen Buddhism, the truth is like the moon floating in the universe. Impossible to touch or grasp. But one can still point at the moon, and this is the function of feeling, rather than words. To Zen, feelings are like words. One of the ways of life in Zen Buddhism is "Ichigo Ichie." Ichigo Ichie means the treasuring of the unrepeatable nature of a moment in life, known as; "for this time only." One will never be in the same place at the same time with the same person ever.

This moment will only happen once in our lives, so put your whole heart into it. In reading this saying, this applies while reading one passage or thought during this one moment in our lives, as it is only going to happen once ever in history. We can come to that same passage or thought in another time in our lives, and it will be another Ichigo Ichie moment in life. This is one reason why we may have another outlook on the same thought we read yearly in our lives.

Another way of life in Zen Buddhism is *"Nichinichi Kurekojitsu."* *Nichinchi Kurekojitsu* means one only has this day, so live it to the fullest. Each day is a great day no matter what hardships may be around us. No two days are the same. All things are unique and irreplaceable. We must learn to embrace each day as if it was our last day. In reading these thoughts, we learn that there is much more than just reading the word, but also understanding them and feeling them. One must keep life simple, yet it may be extremely complex due to the many factors that surround us in life. Understanding that this one moment only comes once in a lifetime.

We must learn to embrace this one moment in life to its fullest, to the point that nothing else matters, just that we are being a part of this life for that one moment. We must remember to stay in tune with what is around us yet be in total emptiness and not think about too much or anything at all.

Equally, we must be still and empty our minds to all thought and or actions in life. This is a very different way of thinking and of being in one's life. However, one must first practice and find balance in order to achieve one's dreams and goals in life. Reading these thoughts is a good step in understanding one's inner self and appreciating every moment in life we have the privilege to experience. Essentially, don't let life get in the way of enjoying life and all its beauty. It only takes five to ten seconds to read one of the thoughts. You will find yourself thinking or reflecting on that thought. How you react to that thought is up to you. You will find out though time, that you will read the same thought and react differently later in life. Don't fear this process as it is life. When we were younger, we learned to feel emotions from experiences in life. Sometimes these experiences are negative and other times, they are positive. Read these thoughts and reflect on them. Embrace those emotions and learn to look deeply into yourselves to find the answer or questions we may have from this thought. The more we practice intersective training, the more we can understand ourselves. Take time to read and understand this thought and how our emotional reflections appear to us. You may find reading the same thought later in life, will have another reflection or even a deeper one from the first one. Remember to embrace your reflections and learn from them.

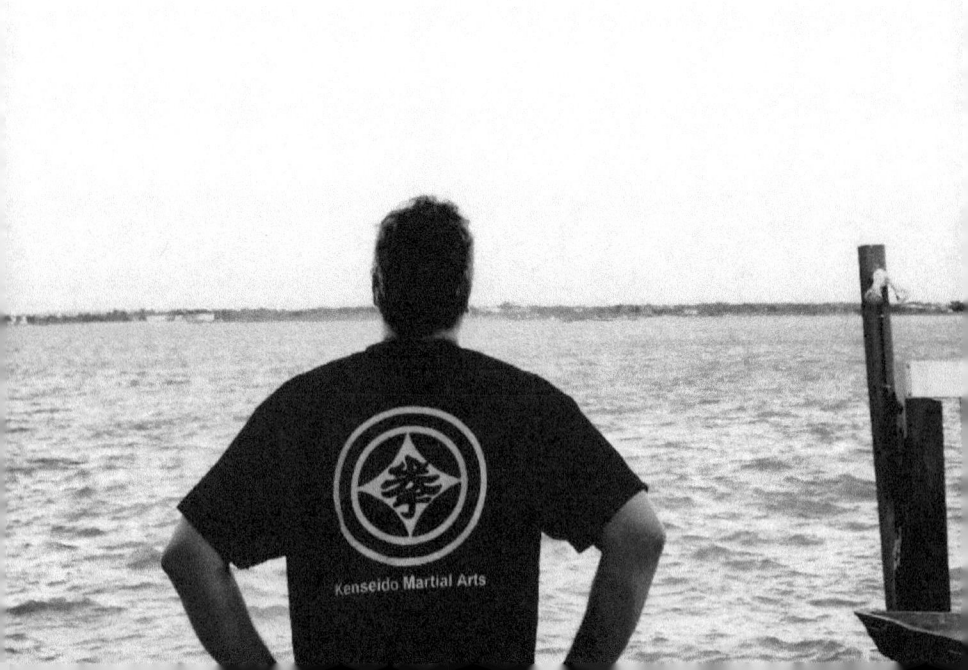

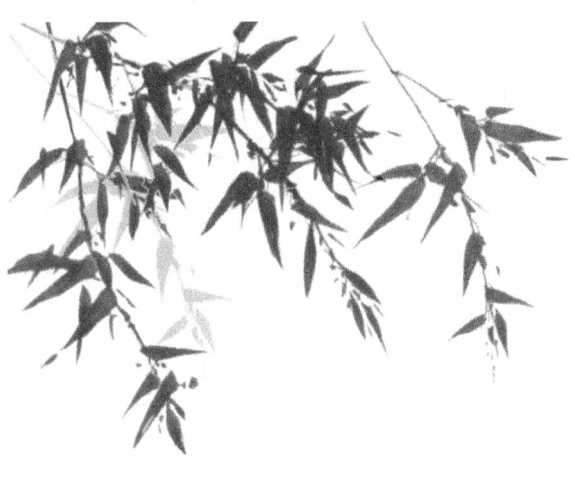

Full Moon on Blue Sky!
Nature tells us anything is possible.

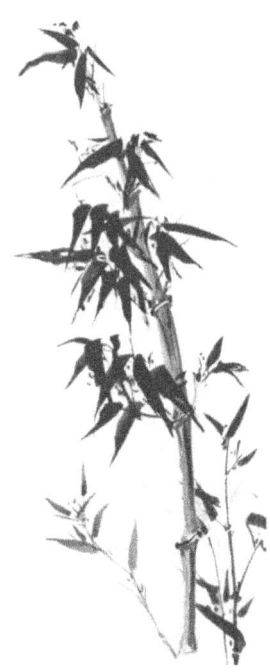

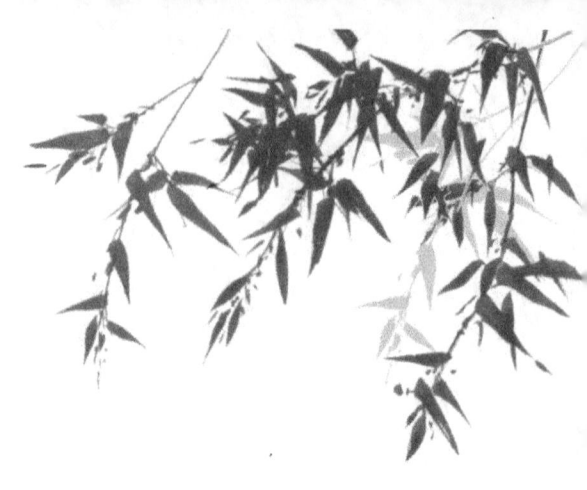

Most try or want to try in life.
But few will overcome and follow through.

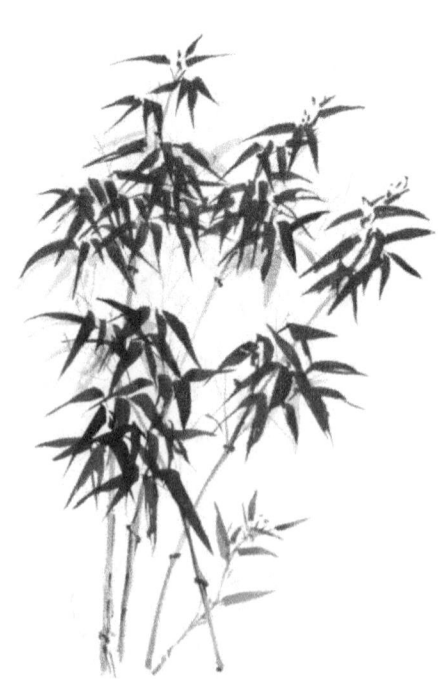

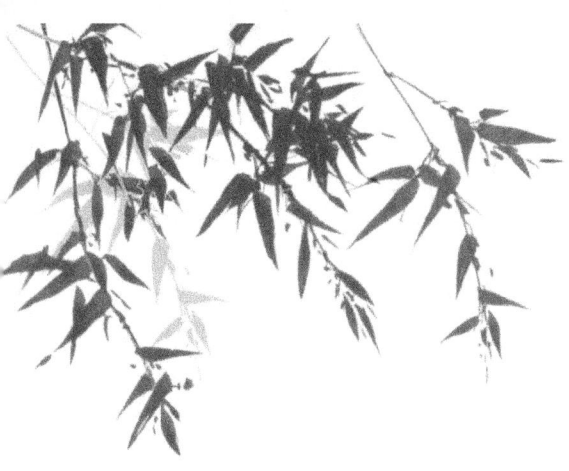

Giving is more rewarding
to a person on the path of enlightenment.
The present molds our future.

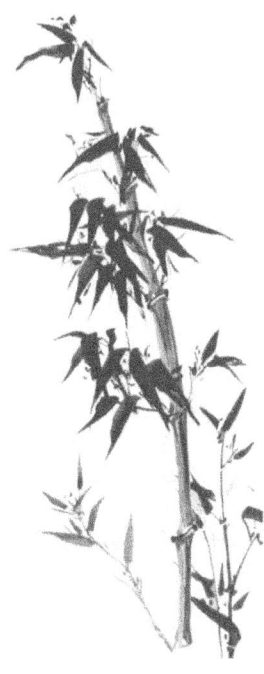

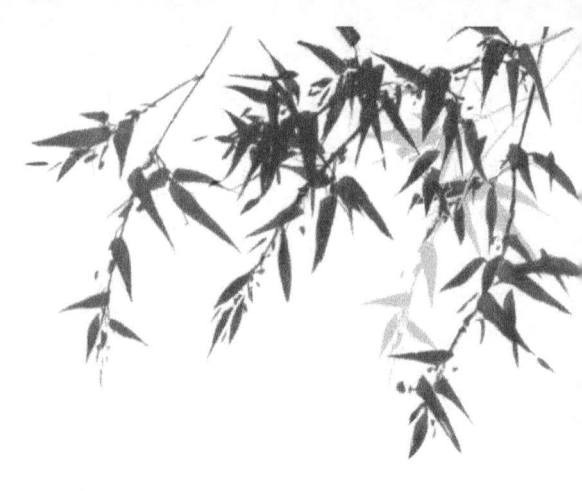

Negative and Positive take the same effort and energy. But are worlds apart.

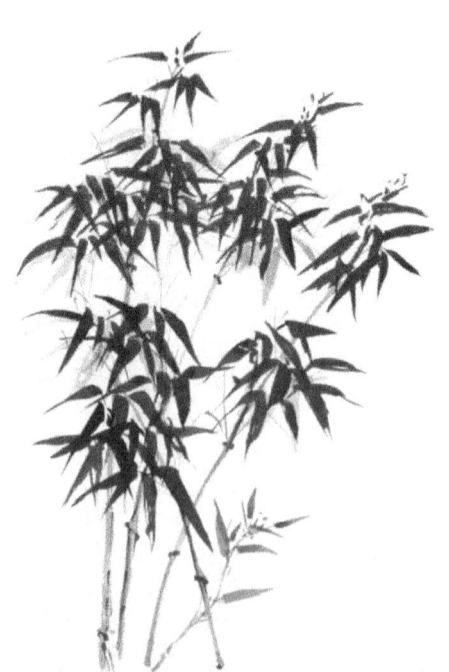

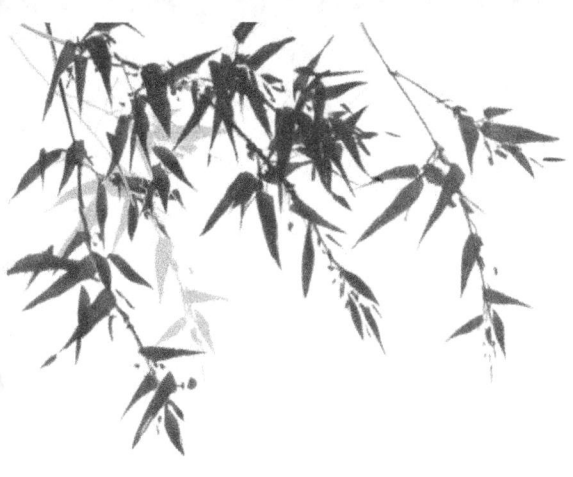

Knowledge and wisdom are different.
Much as trees and the ground.

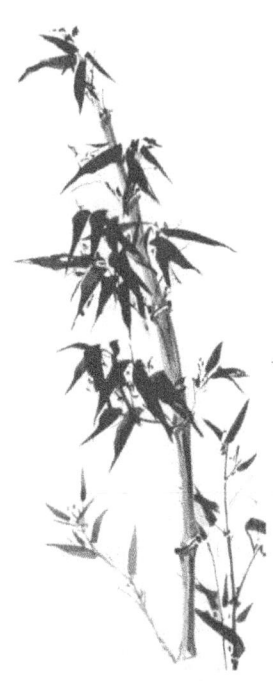

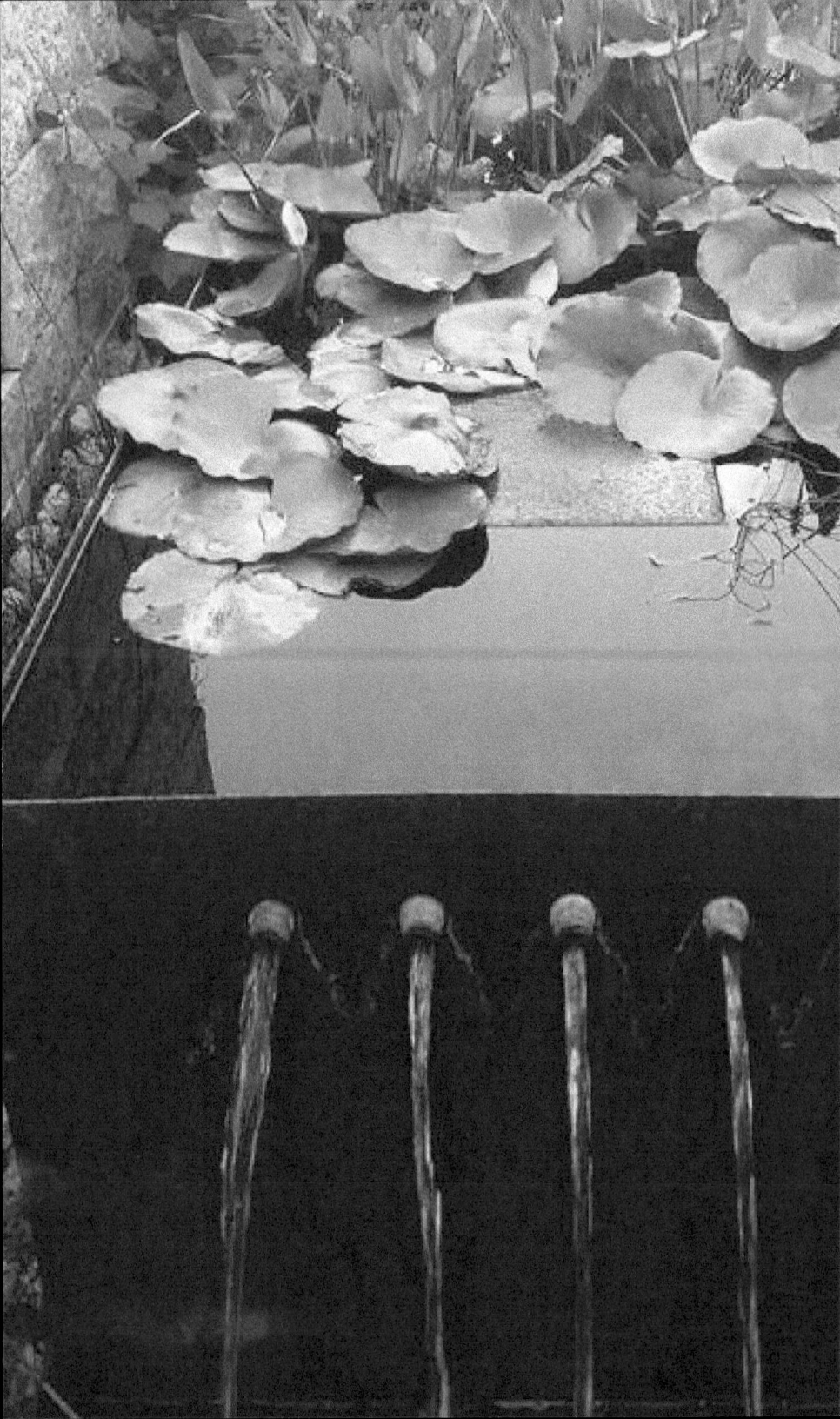

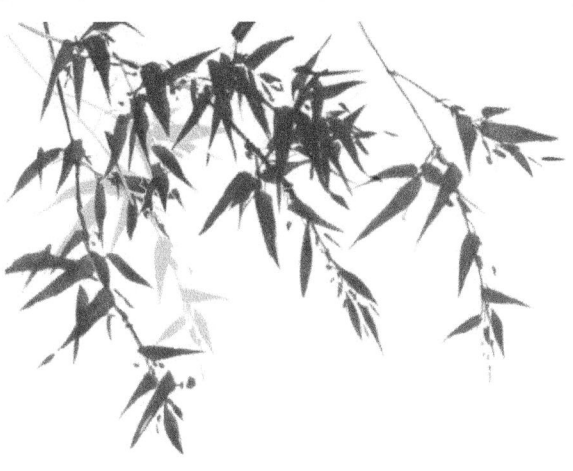

If one wants to work on self.
One must first look at the water.

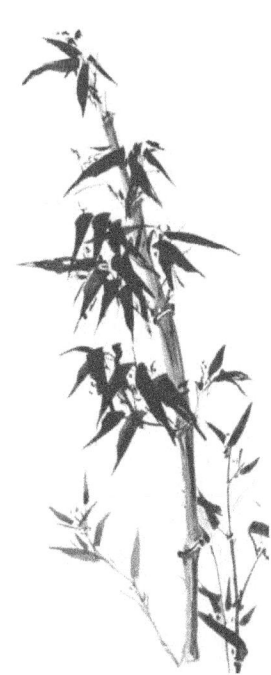

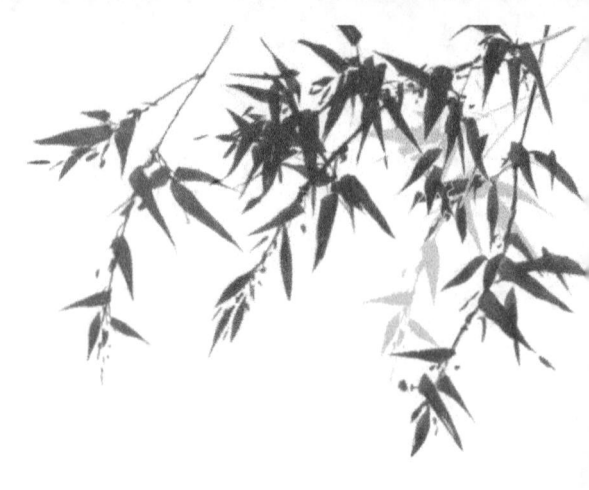

In a perfect world
there will be no need to lie.

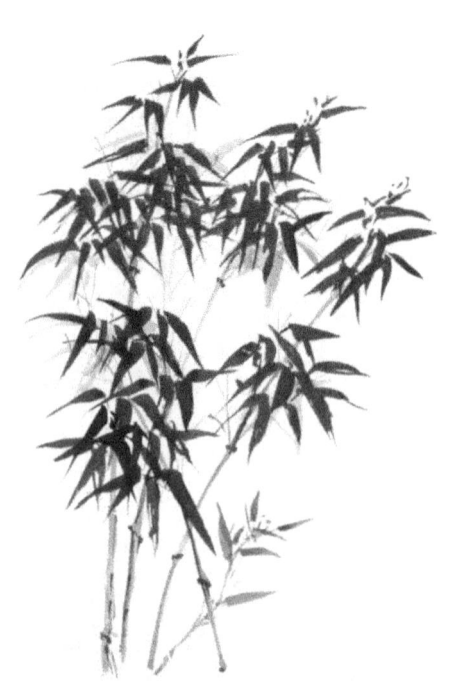

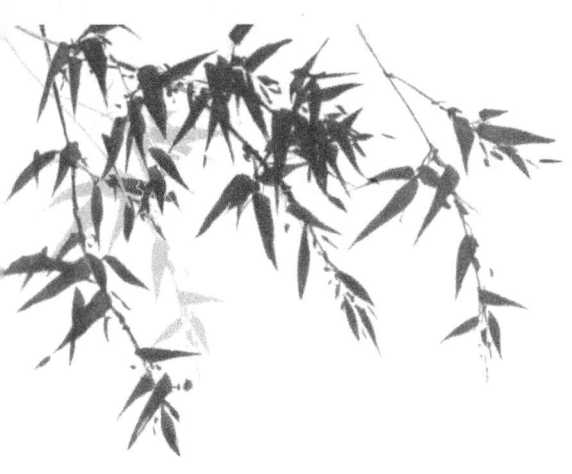

Humans are Complex.
Life is Simple.
Humans are Simple.
Life is Complex.

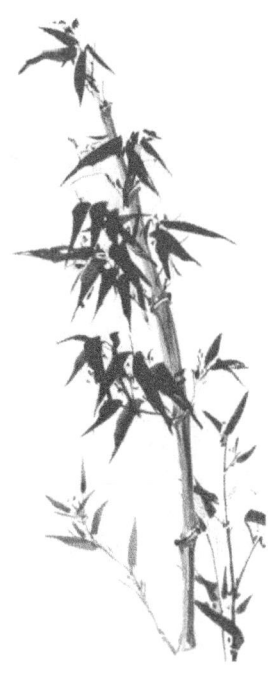

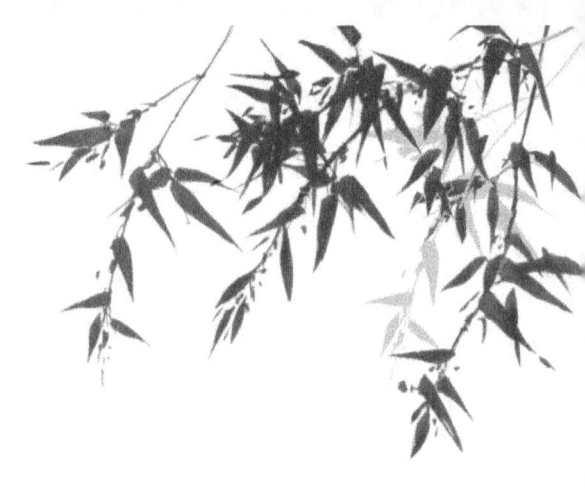

If one is not happy with self.
Then one cannot hear one's own heartbeats.

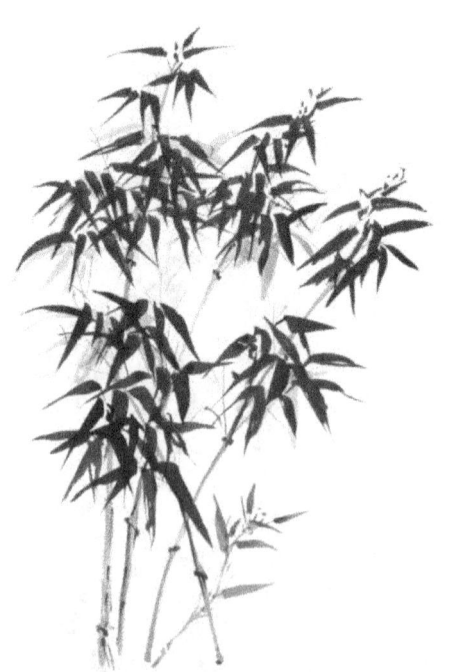

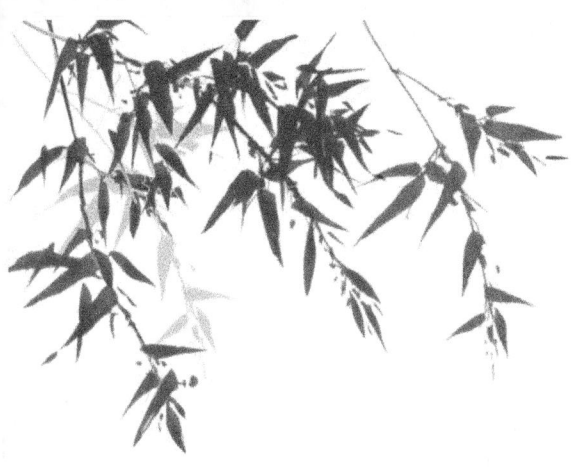

Who is to blame for war?

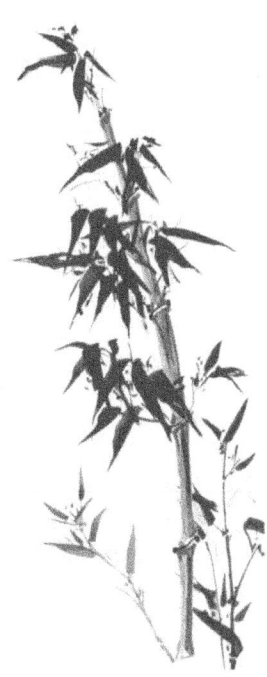

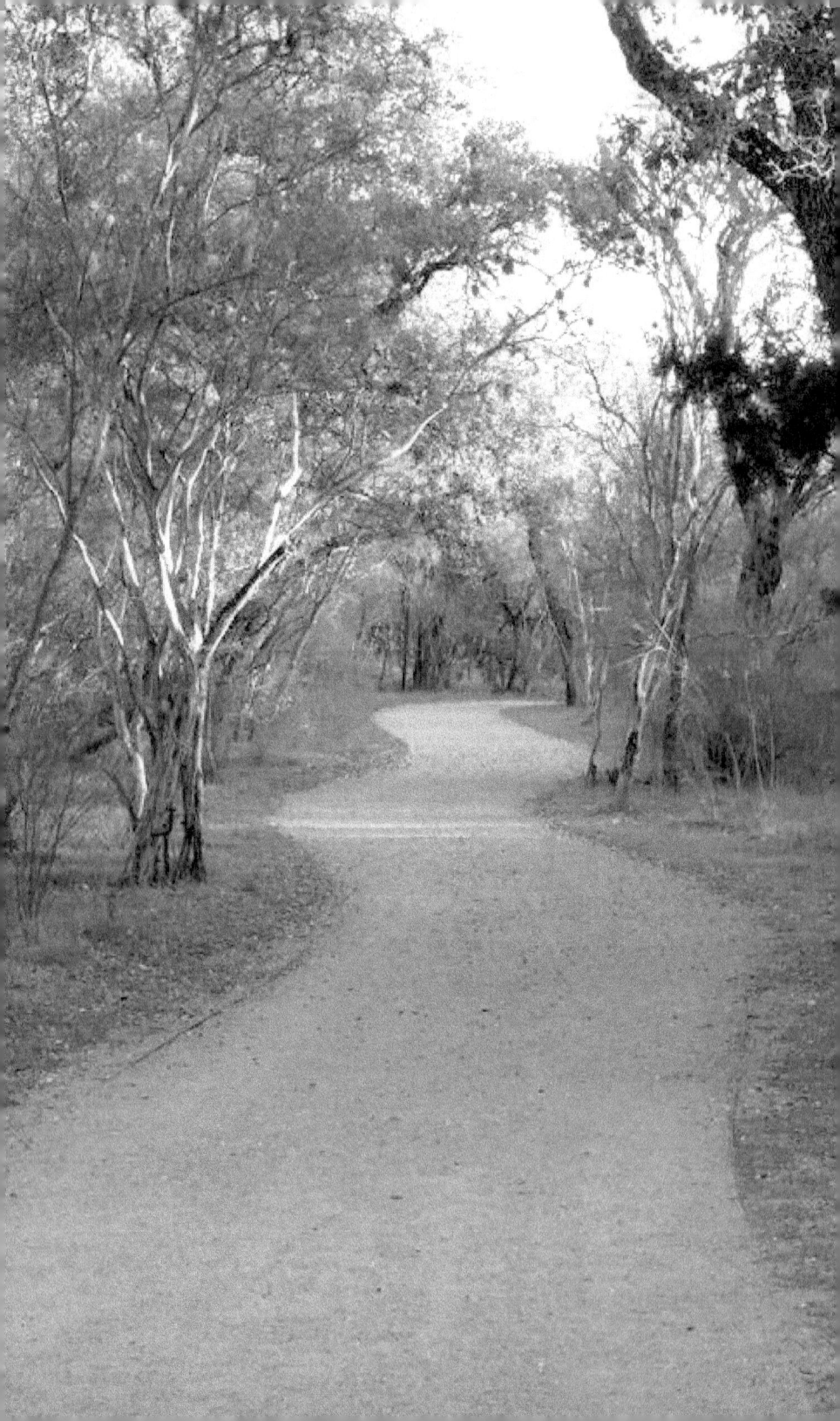

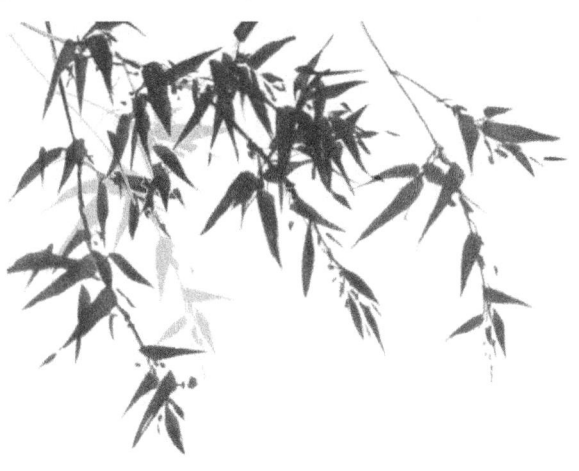

The Path
is a Path
on a Path.

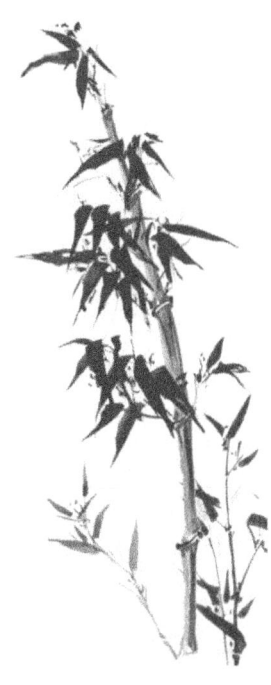

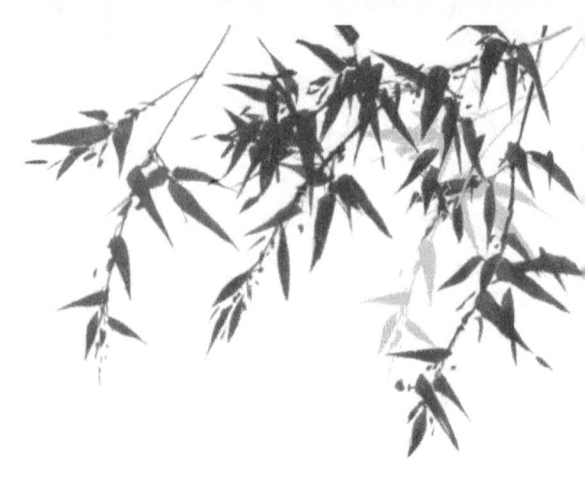

The difference between good and bad deeds
is a matter of one's point of view.

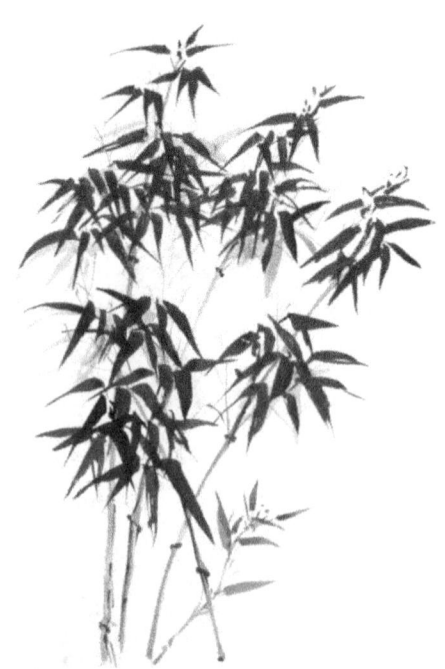

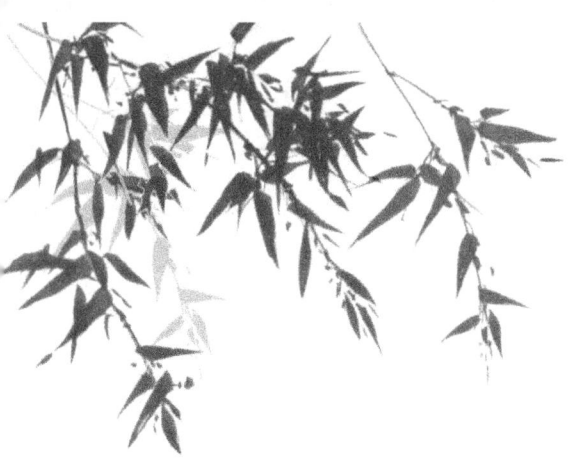

A strong spirit (Kokoro),
can bridge any lands.

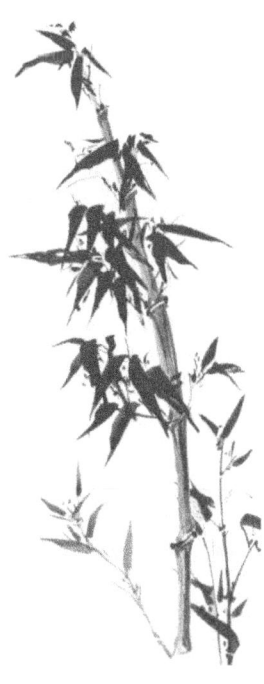

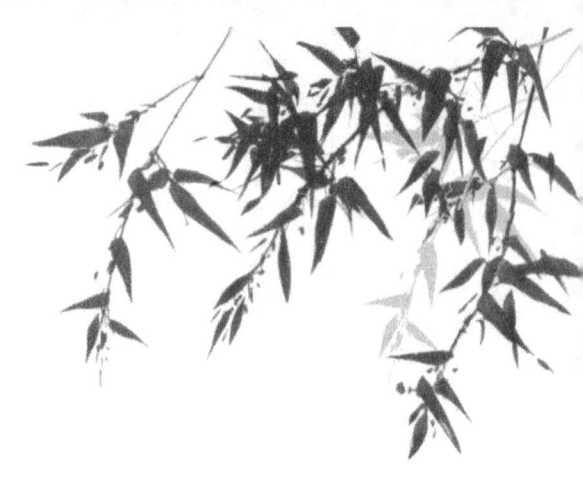

Light is good and dark is bad.
Not to a thief.

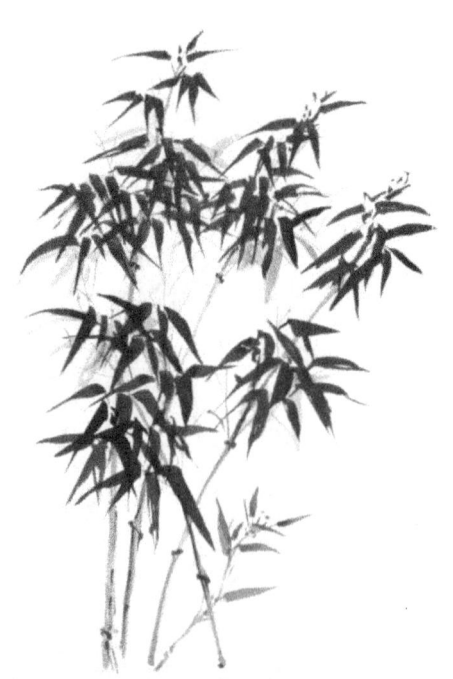

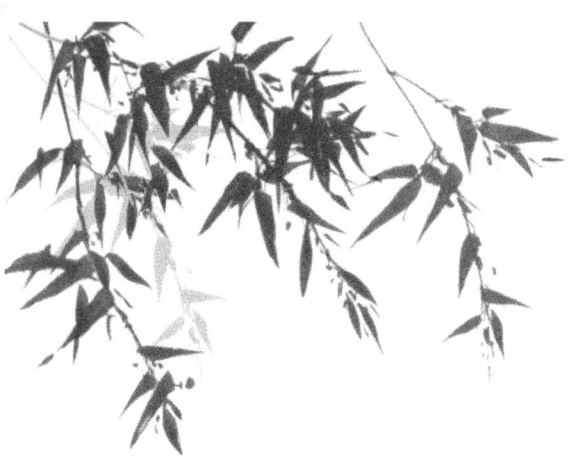

My will aches for peace.
My heart aches for enlightenment.
My spirit aches for the journey.

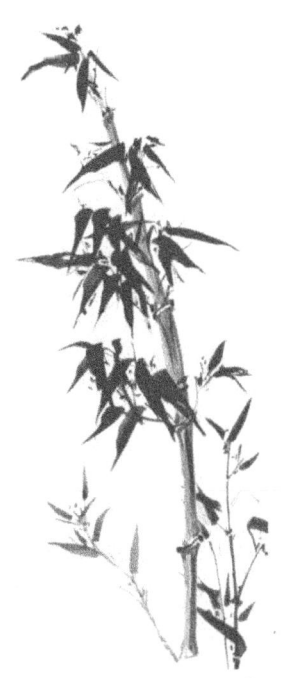

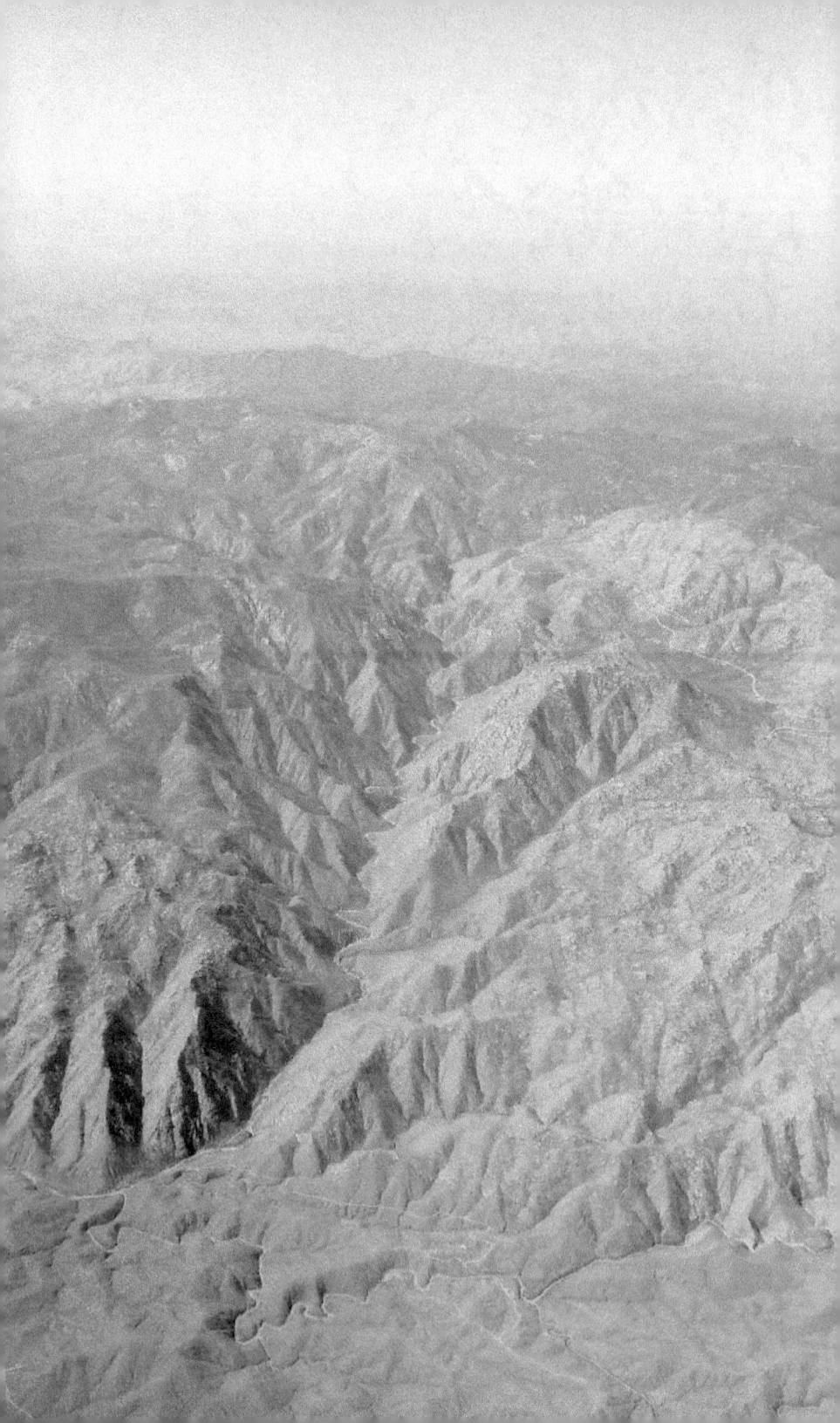

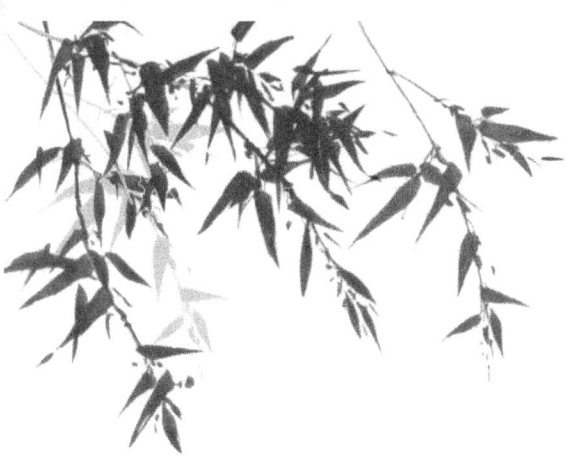

Spirit + Heart + Emotion = Music

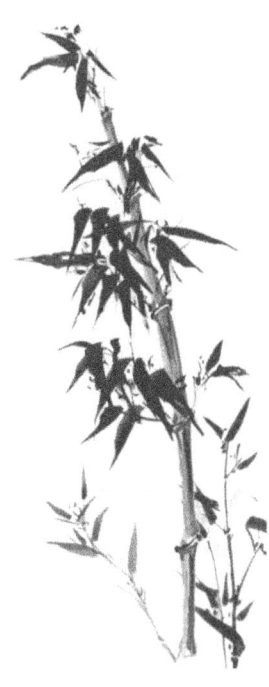

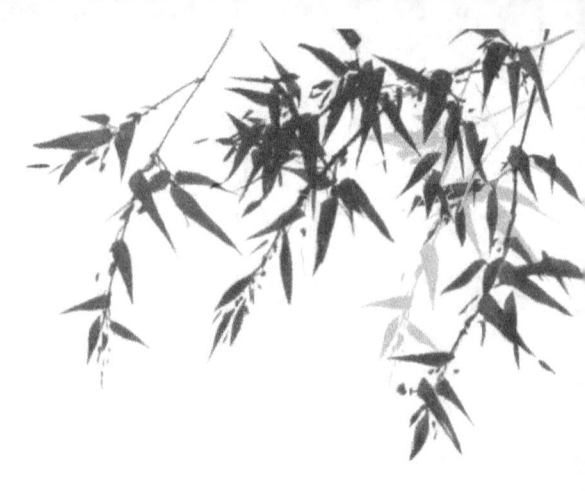

Humans are creatures of habit.
Habits can be powerful and flawed,
much as humans.

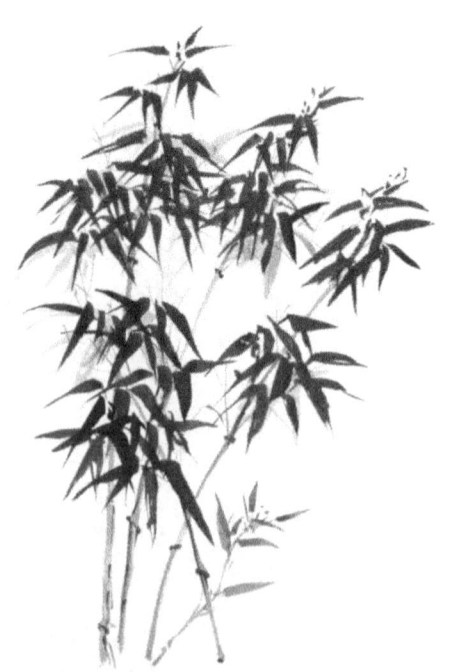

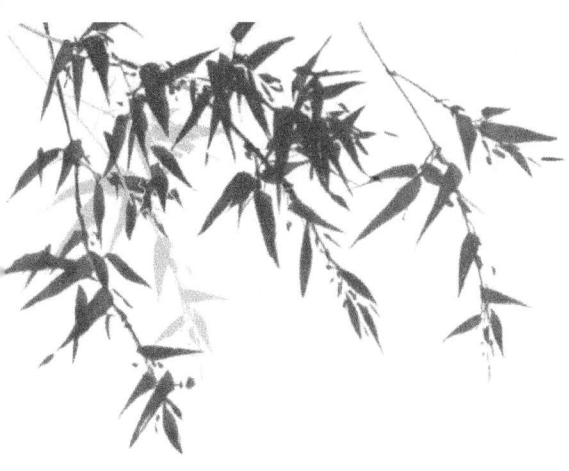

If the truth is truly spoken,
then it is an errorless conversation.

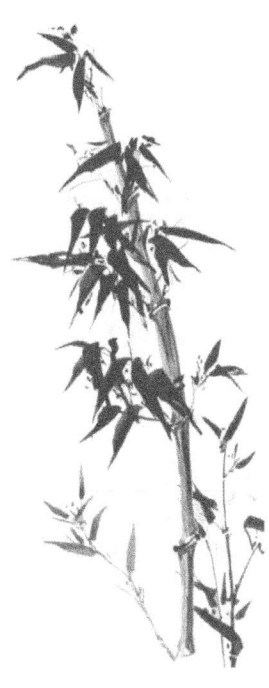

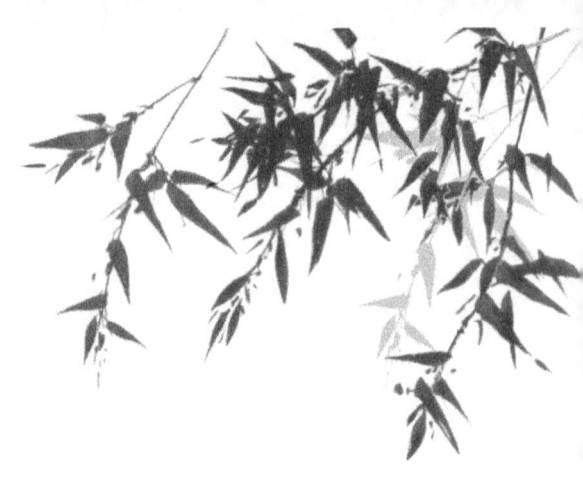

Martial Arts is much like the universe.
Vast and limitless.

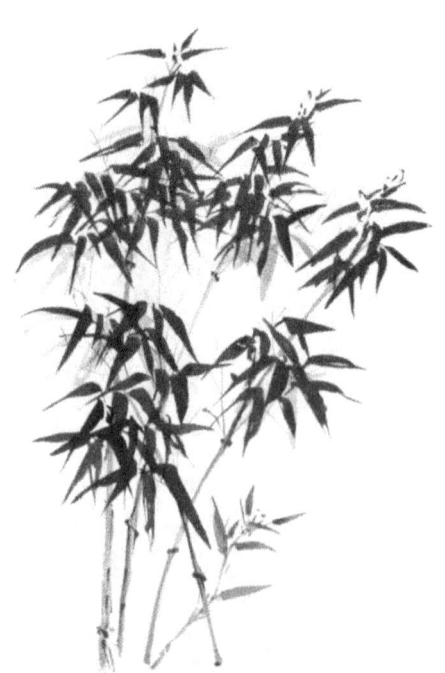

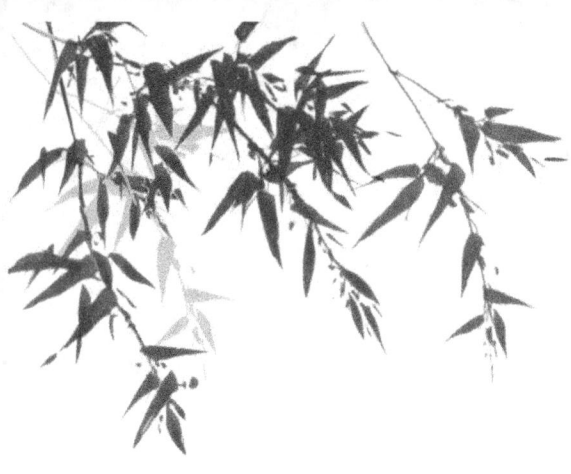

Wind flows though a flute caressing the ear.
The path is the echoes.

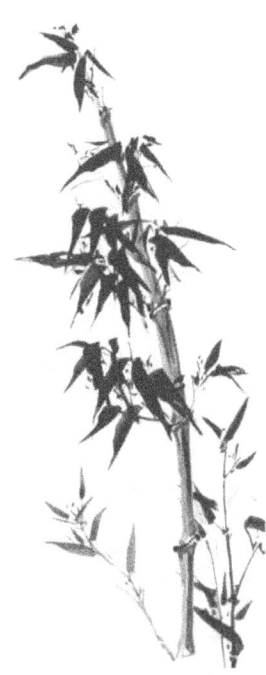

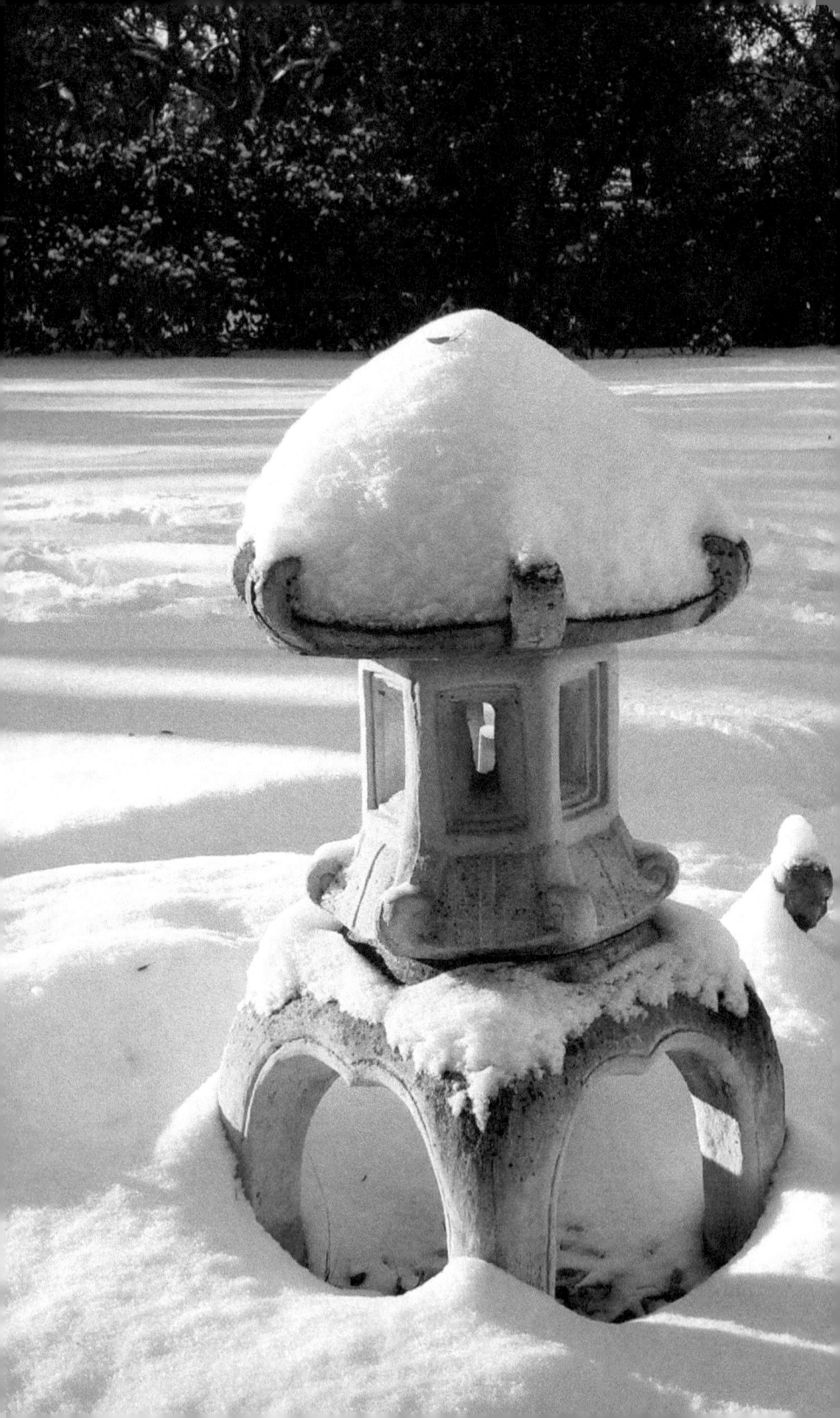

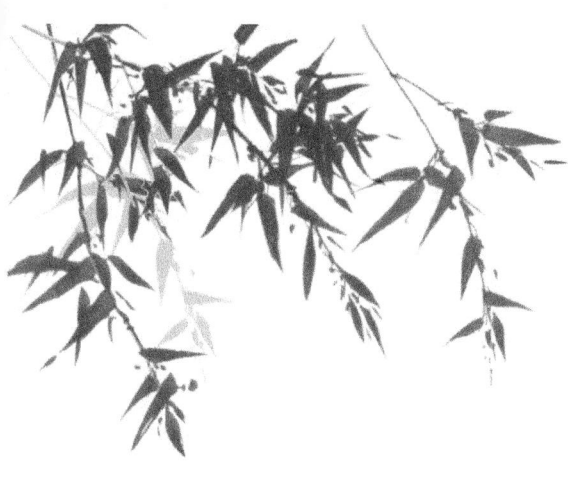

If the world had no music.
What then.

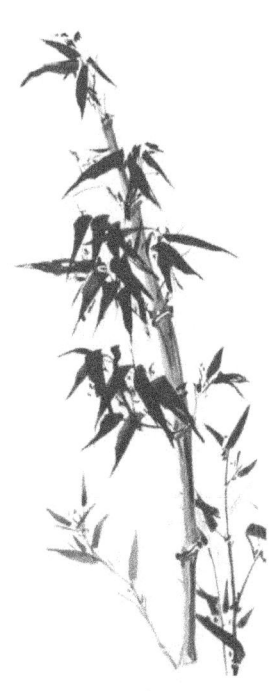

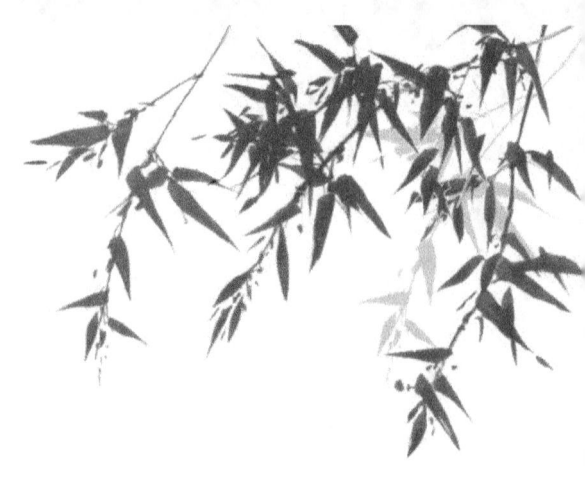

As the sun rises from the edge,
its warmth caresses everything
but the shadows.

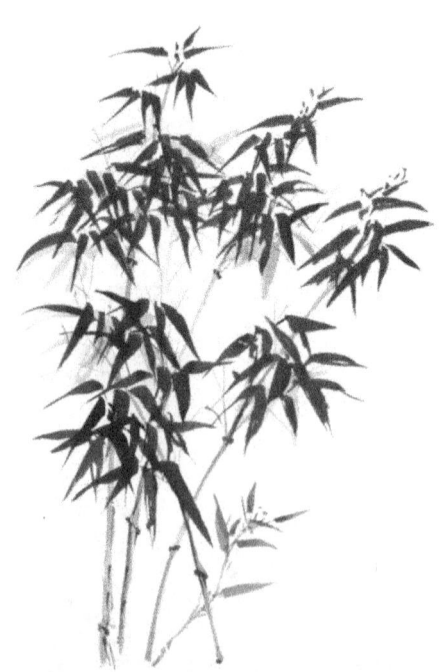

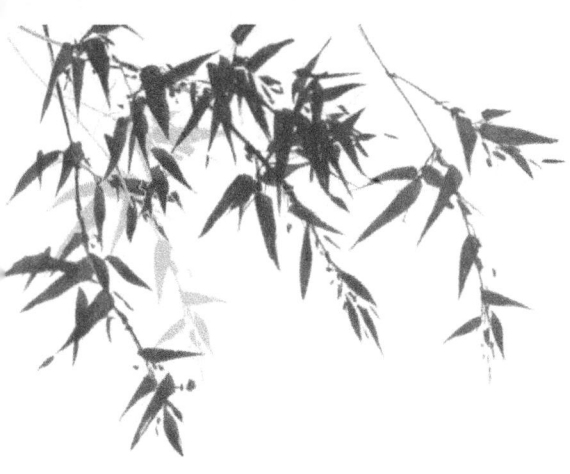

Strong body and weak spirit
can be as strong as a train wreck.

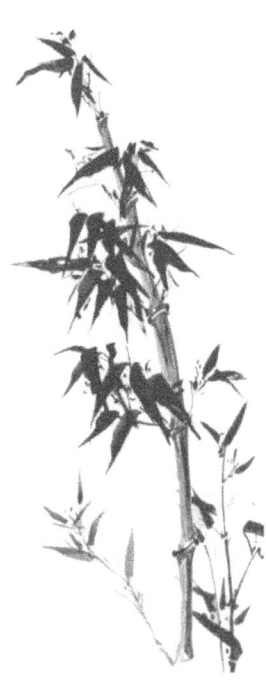

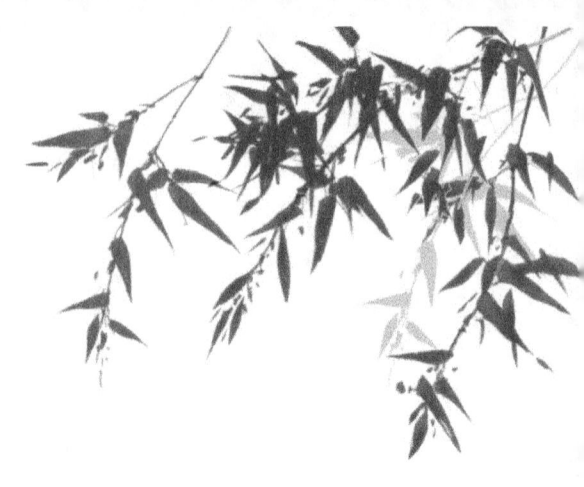

The universe has rules.
One must have knowledge of these rules
in order to find balance in life.

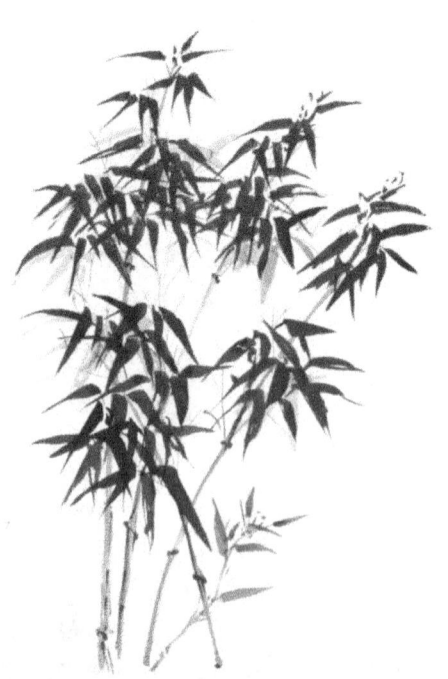

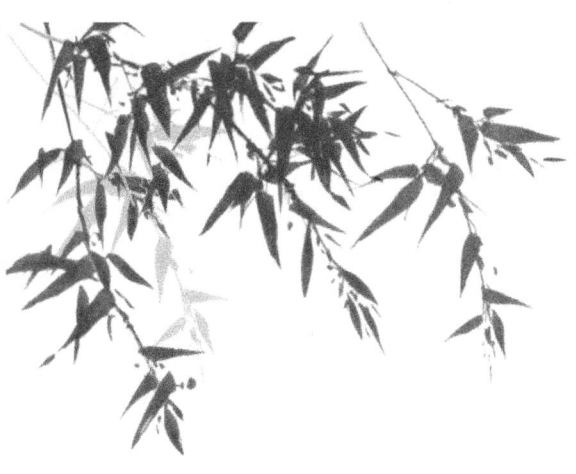

With time a penny dropped into the ocean
will tarnish.
Humans that drop their lives into negativity
will tarnish too.

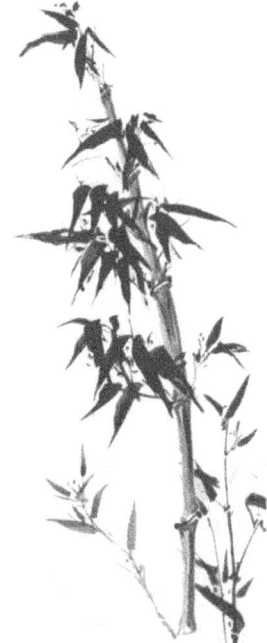

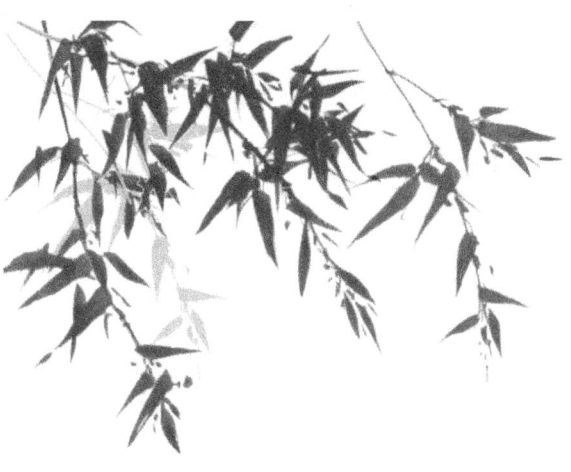

If one's life is not positive,
then walk though the mirror
and shatter negativity.

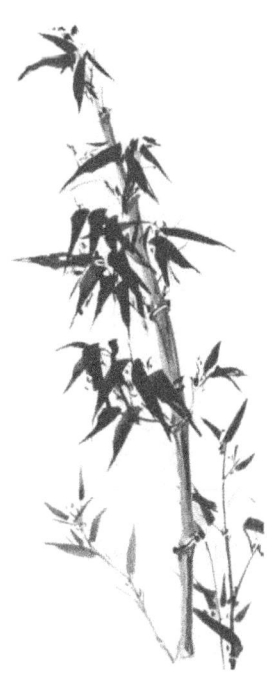

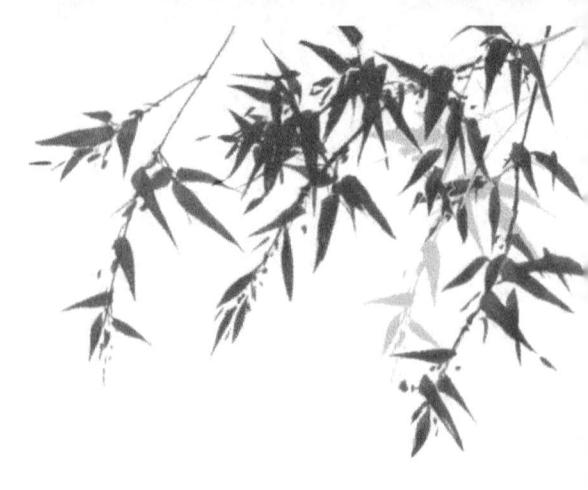

Who stole the child's lollipop?
Look for a politician.

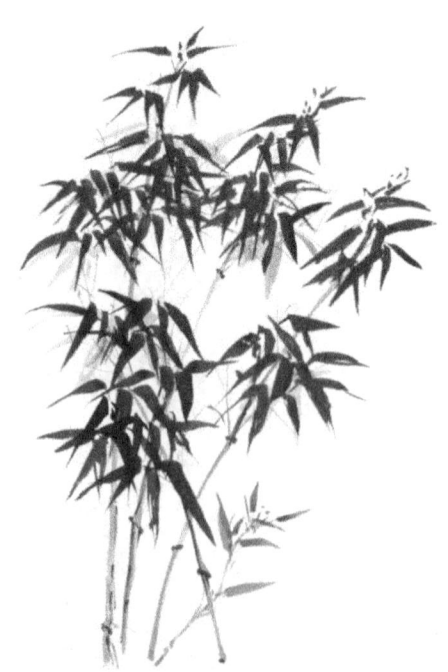

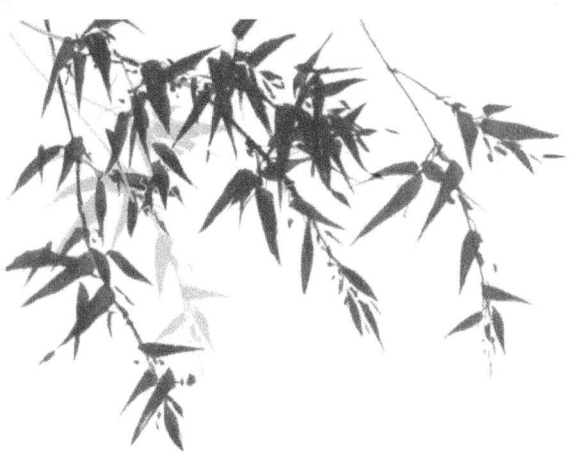

Tears fell down like flowers pedals in spring.

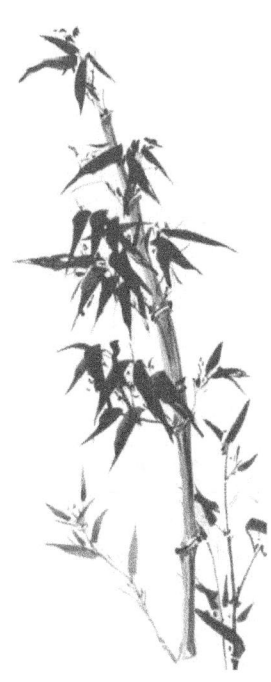

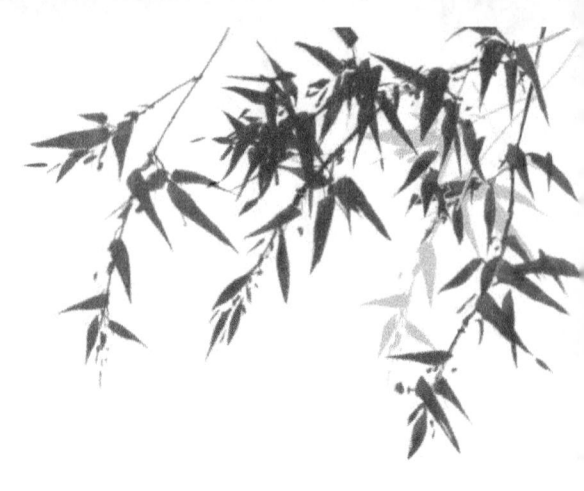

A good teacher must
also be good student.

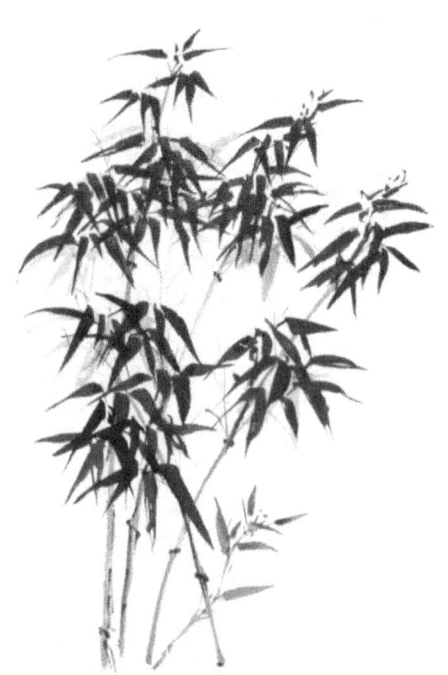

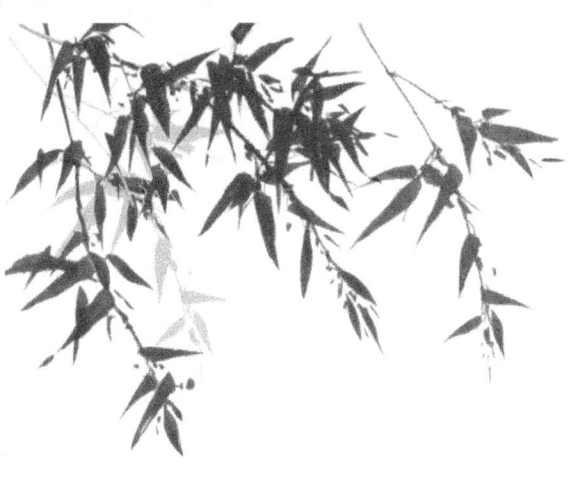

The path of life has many ways.
But only one is true.

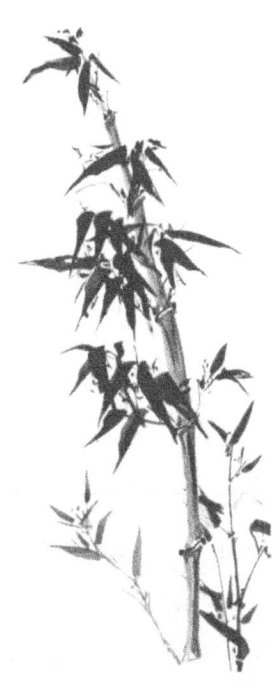

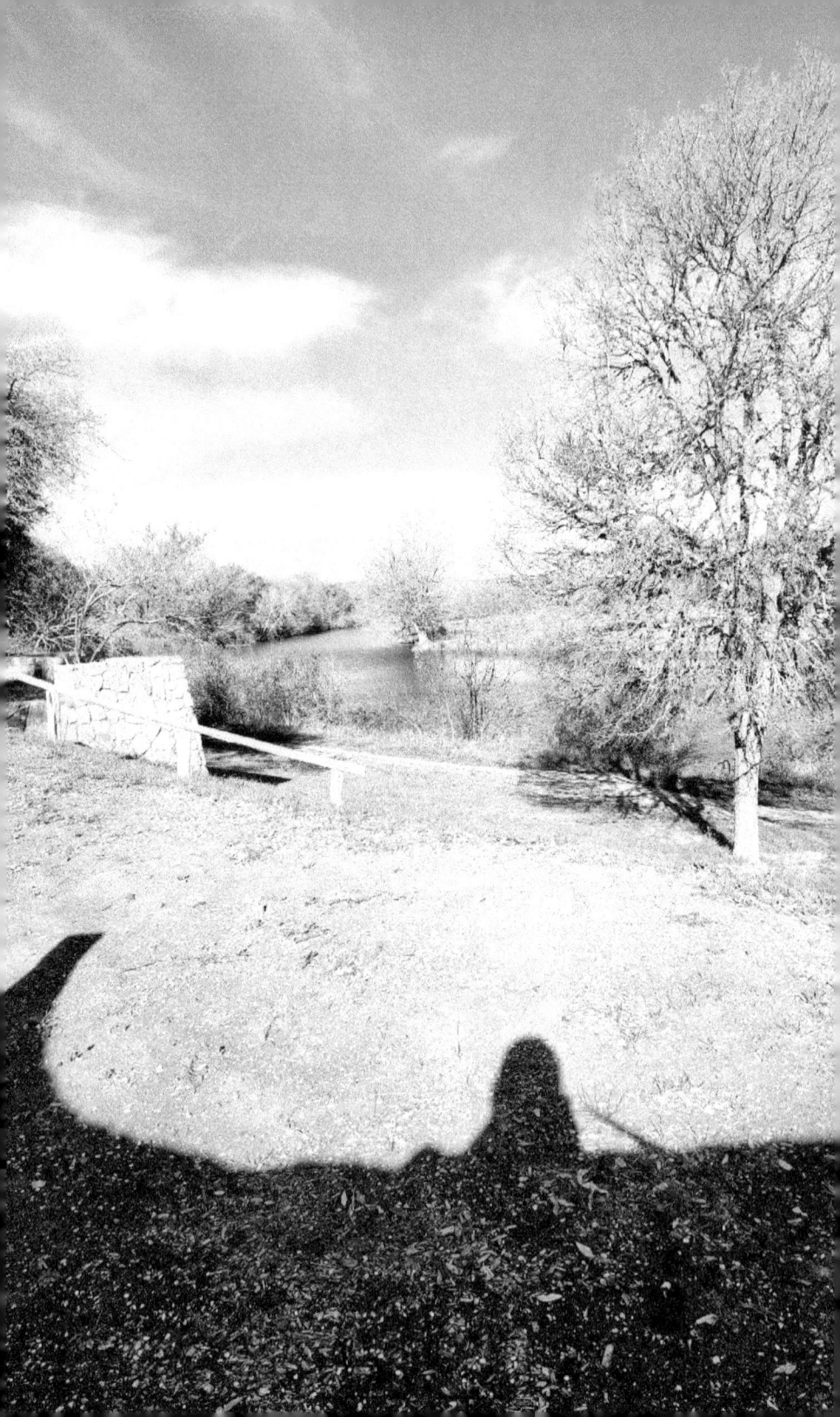

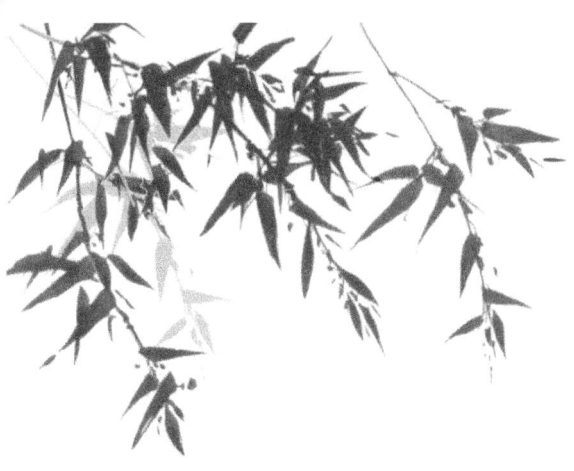

If one needs to find balance in life,
one must first find peace within.

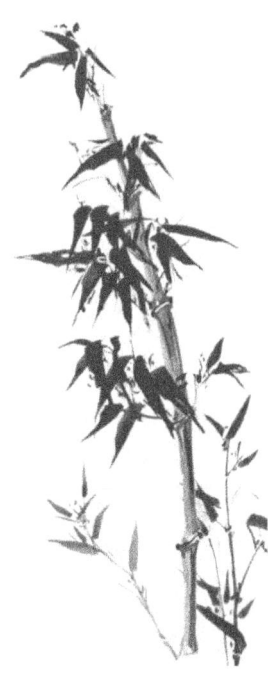

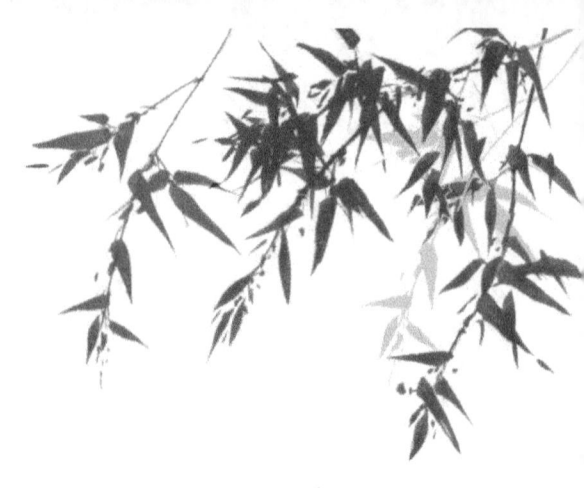

One must remember
the media would like us to believe their point of view
all in the name of greed.

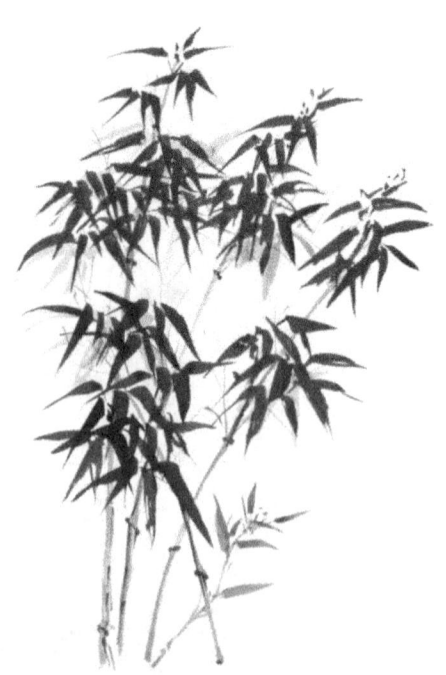

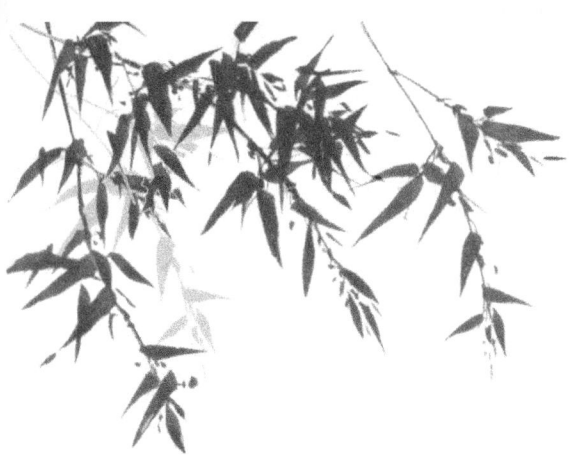

Children are great observers in life.
Adults are great lecturers in life.
Which is more balanced and powerful?

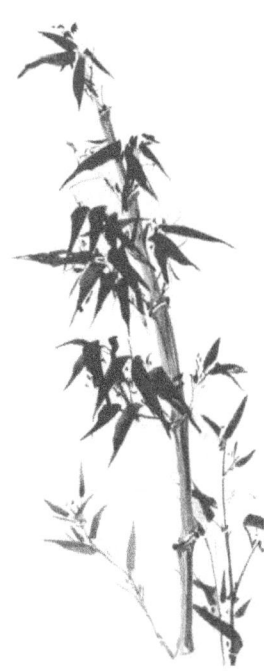

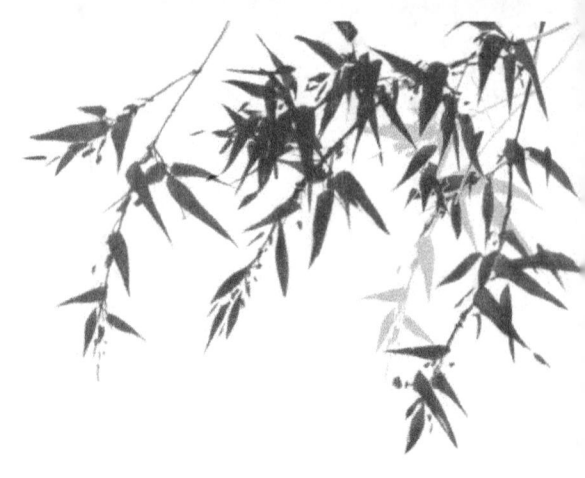

War is the bureaucrat's way of
disagreement and malice.
Jail is the citizen's way of
disagreement and malice.

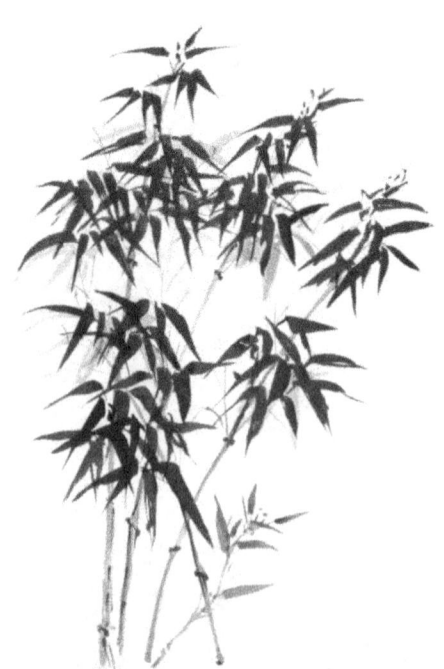

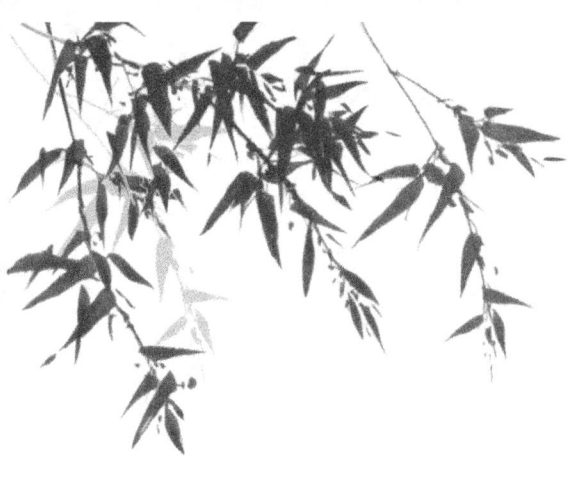

A pebble dropped into a pond
ascends into a new life.

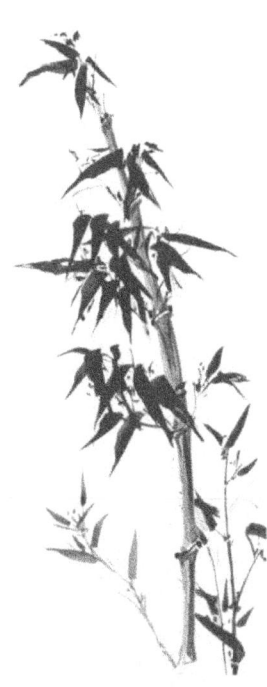

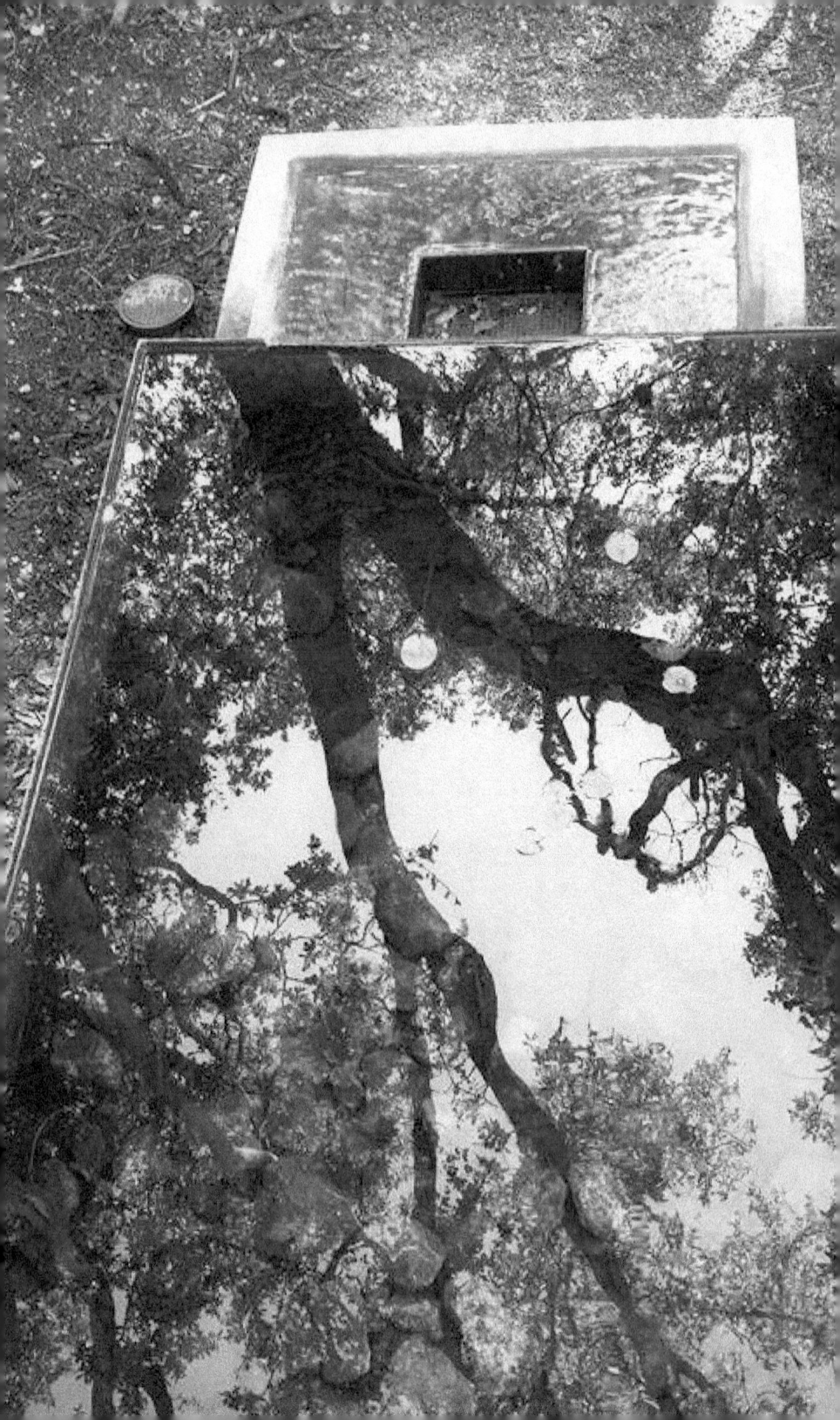

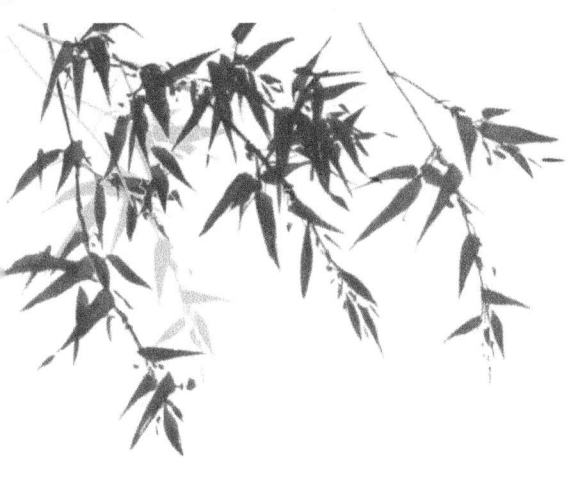

If one eats too much, one feels overextended.
The key is to have moderation in life.

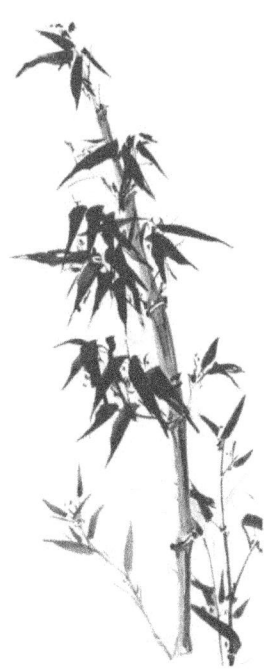

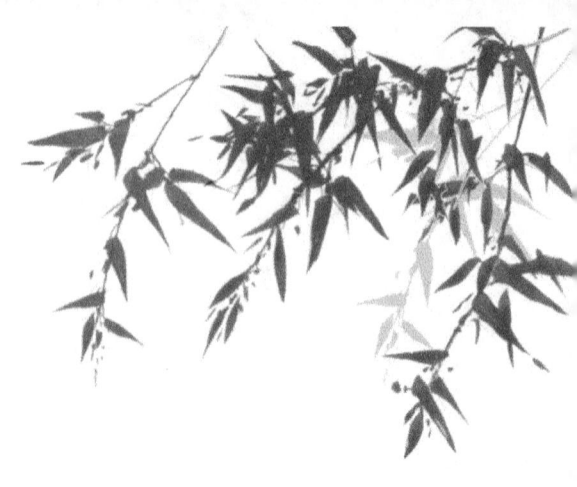

Out of the ashes comes life,
end of life starts a new life.
What a mysterious life we live in.

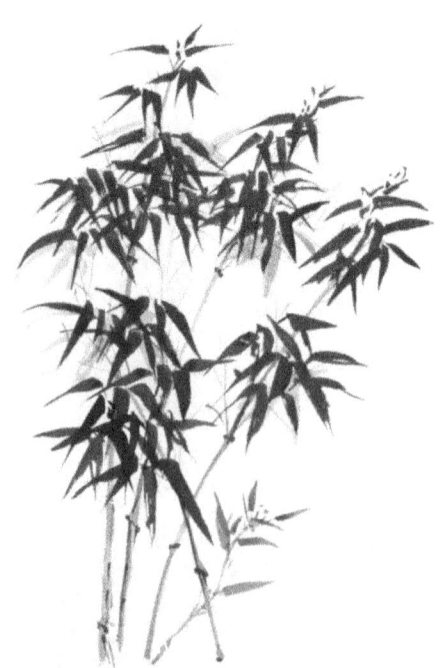

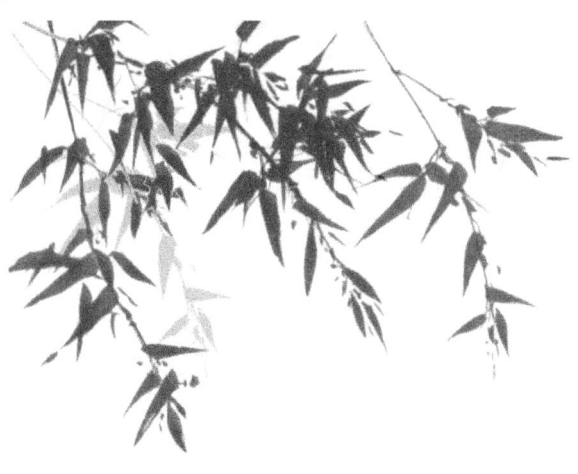

Blue skies and black holes.
The lilies lie gently on the pond.
Life is grand if one knows what to look for.

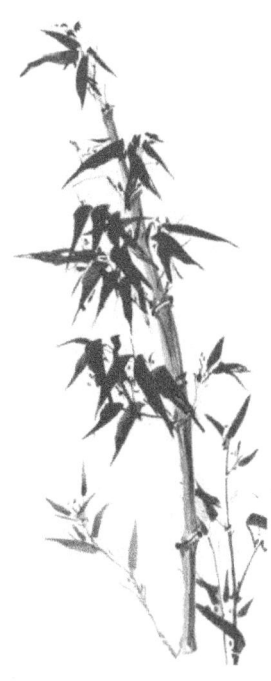

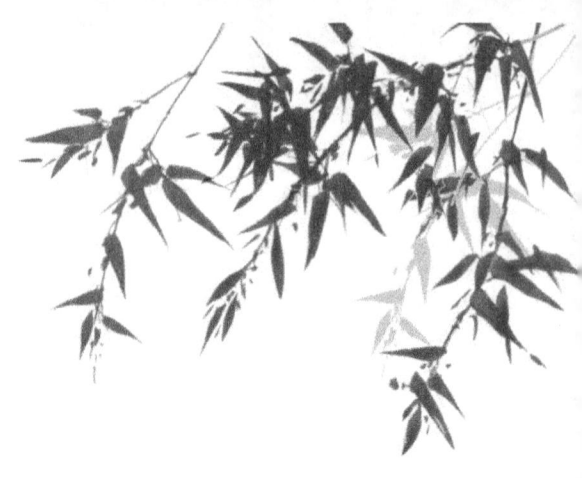

In order for one to find and be balanced in life.
One must be able to:

See the beauty of life.
Smell the beauty of life.
Hear the beauty of life.
Taste the beauty of life.
Feel the beauty of life.

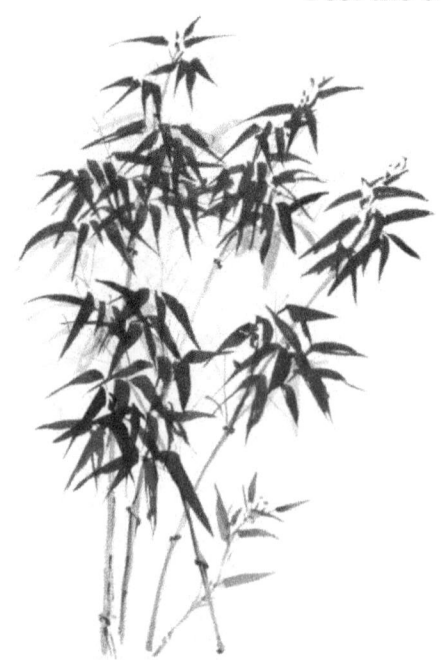

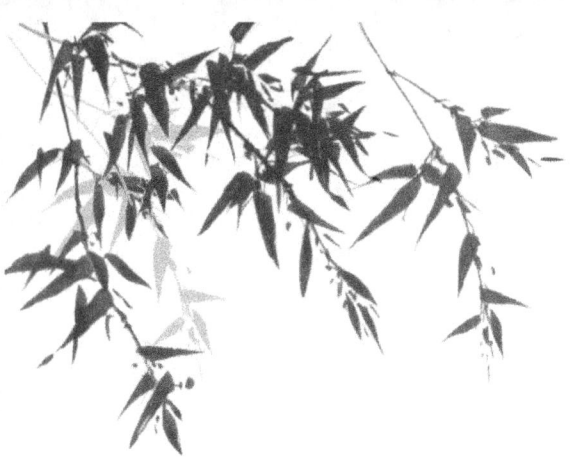

The dim light curls the toes.
Clearing the mind.
Beauty lies within.

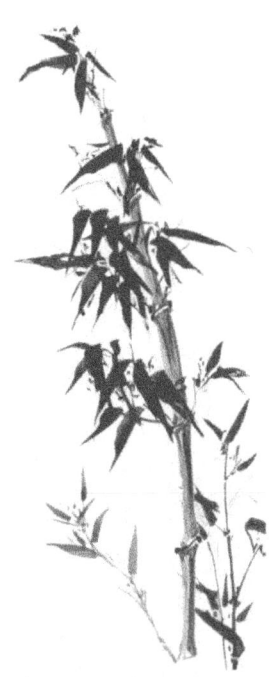

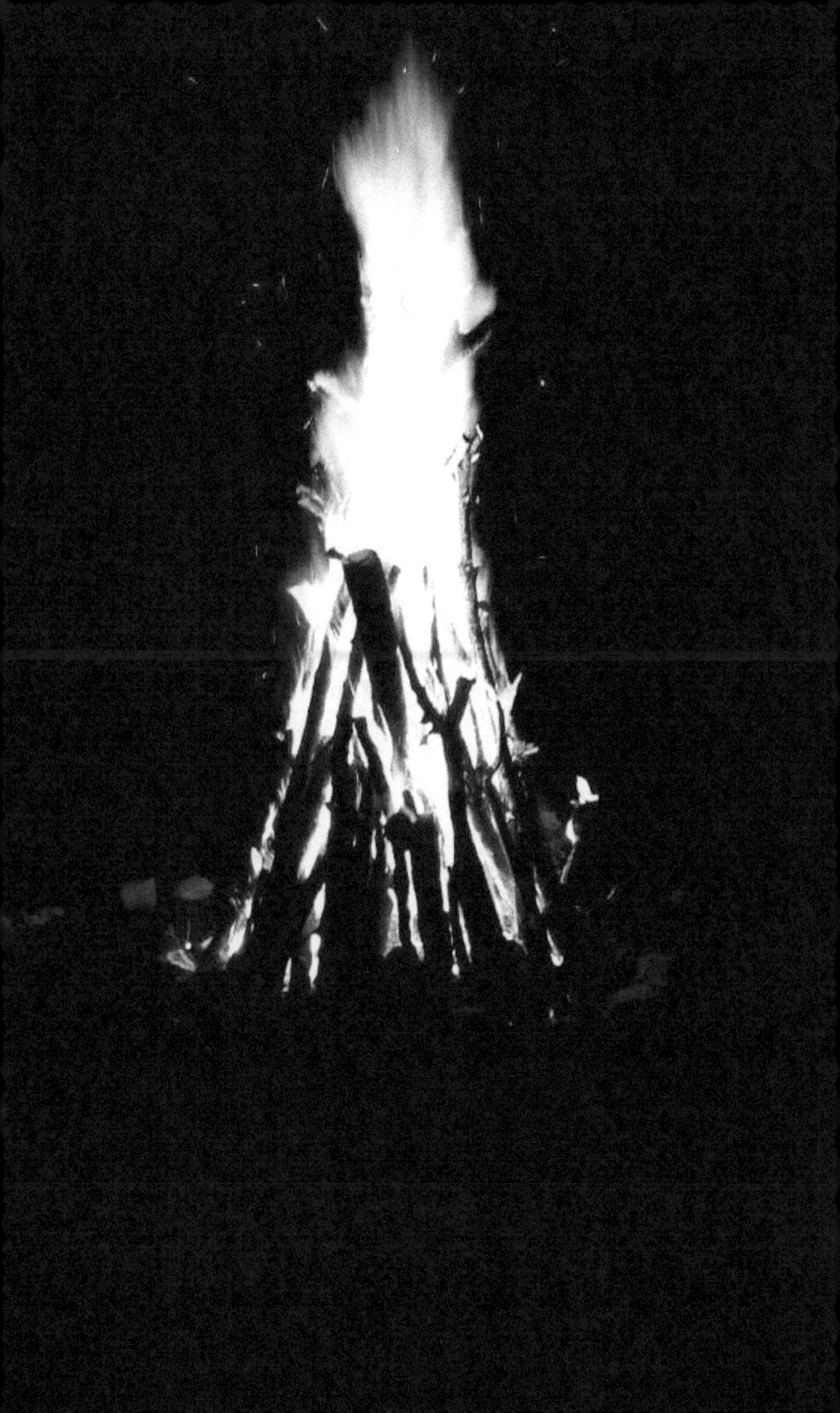

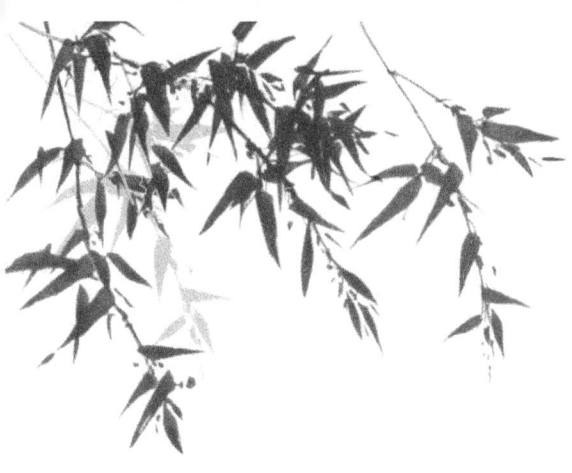

As the full moon rises, some creatures go to bed.
For others, it's the start of a new life.

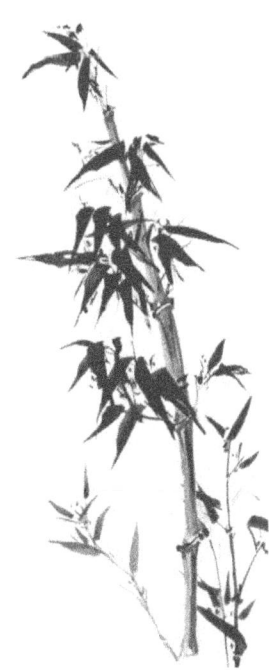

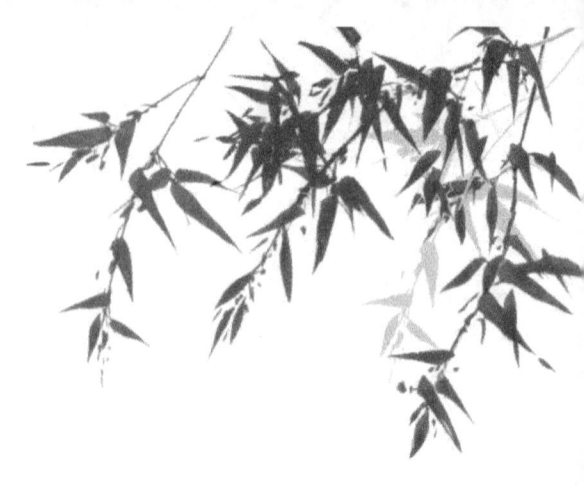

Full moon on clear sky,
the effects can be intoxicating.

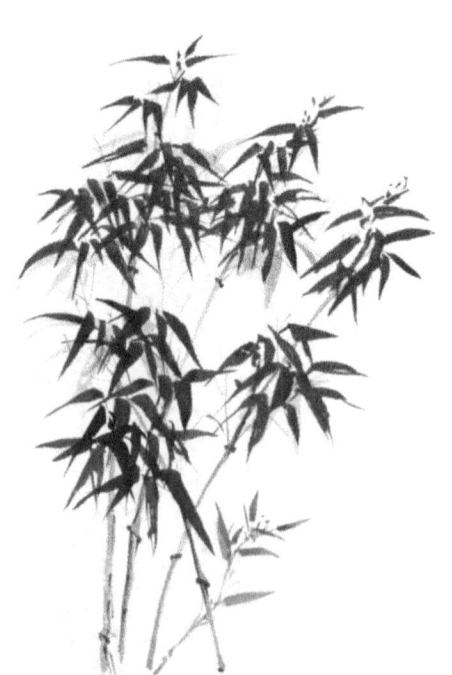

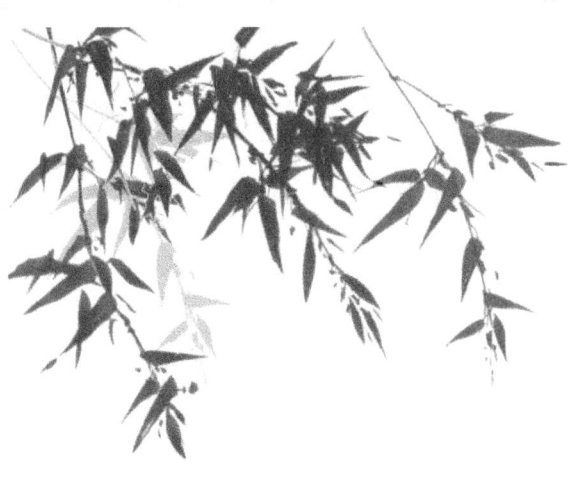

Life is grand.
When one can learn to deal with lives stress properly.

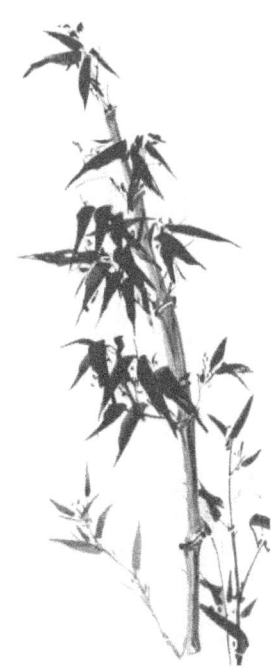

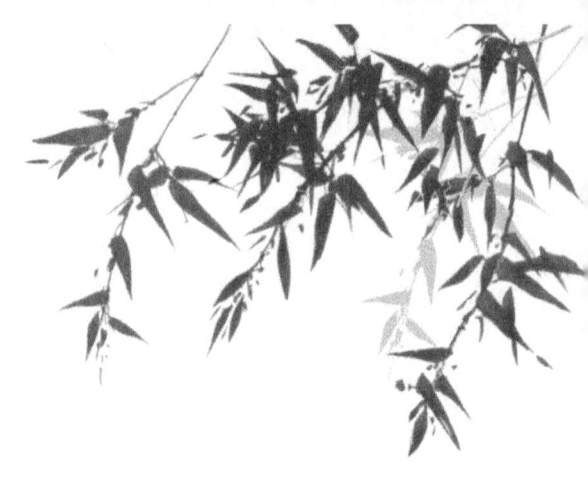

Movies are fantasy!
Life is reality!

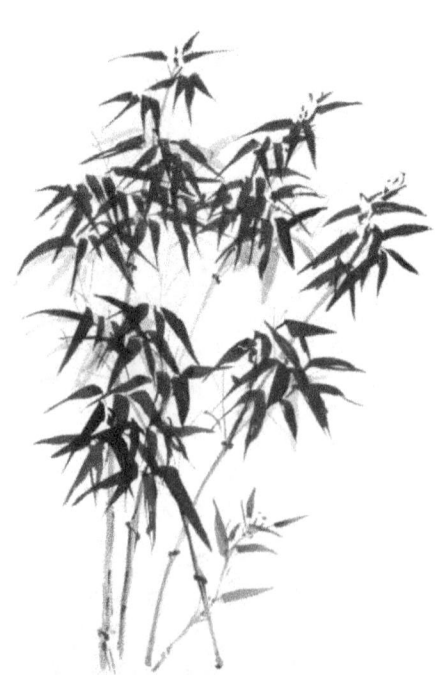

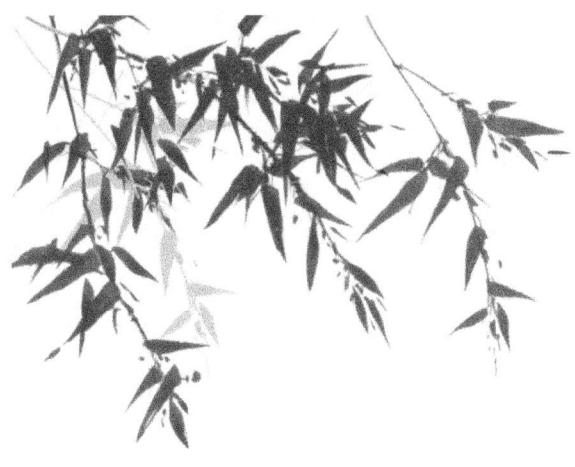

Breathe.........
Focus..........
Live............
Enjoy........

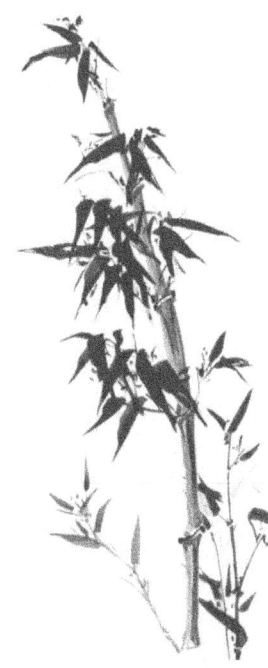

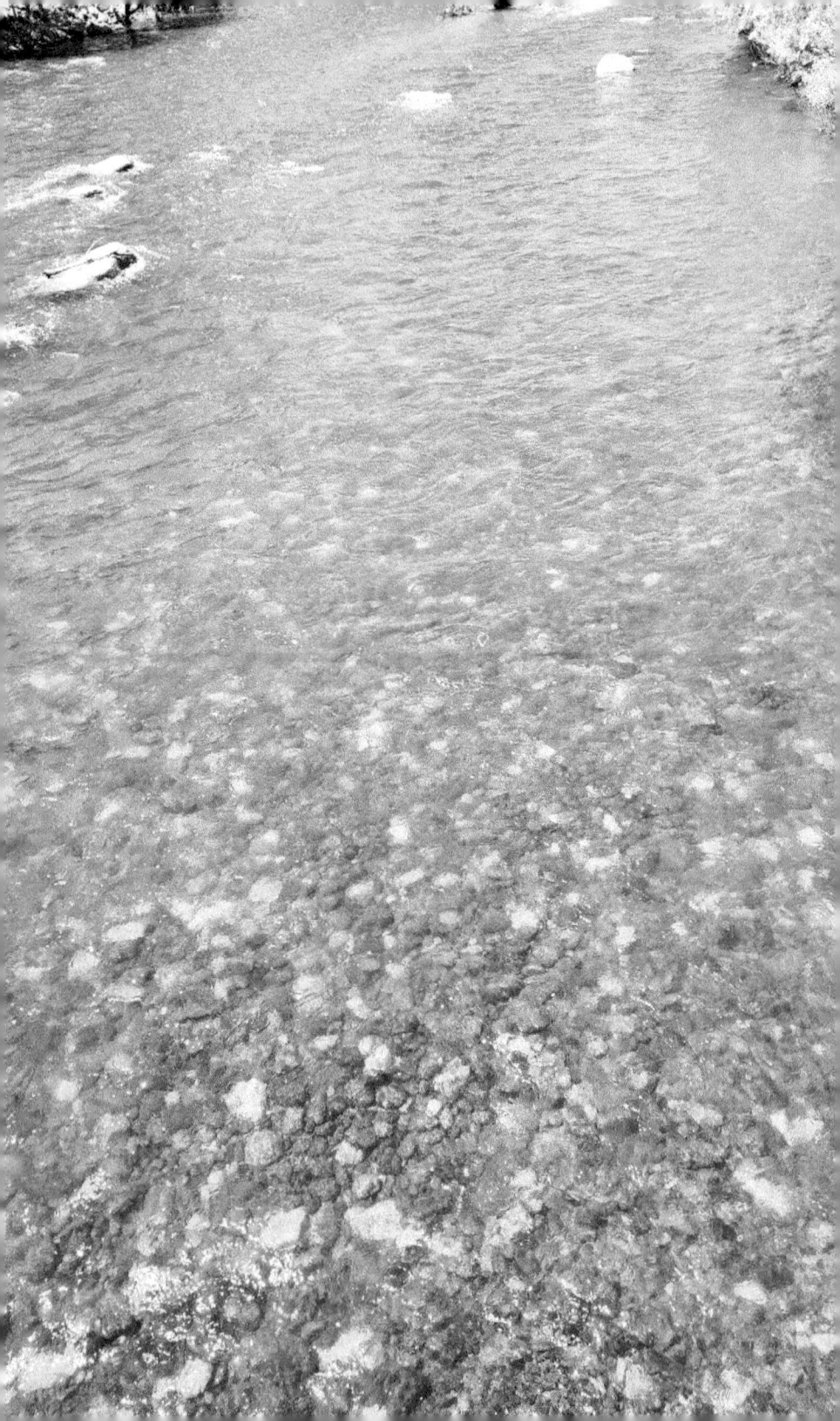

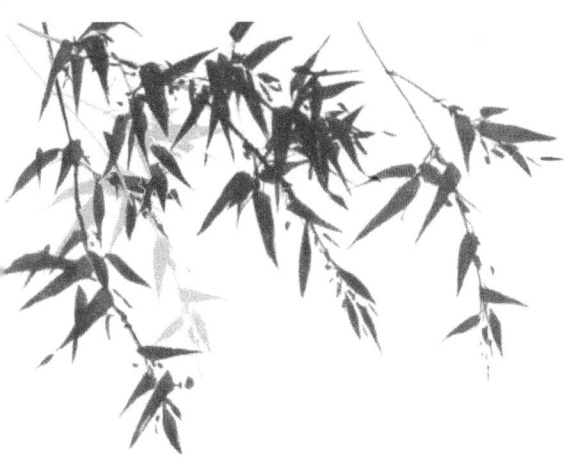

The dirt on your shoes are reminders of our past.

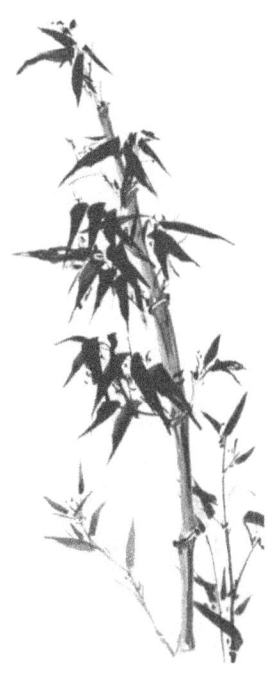

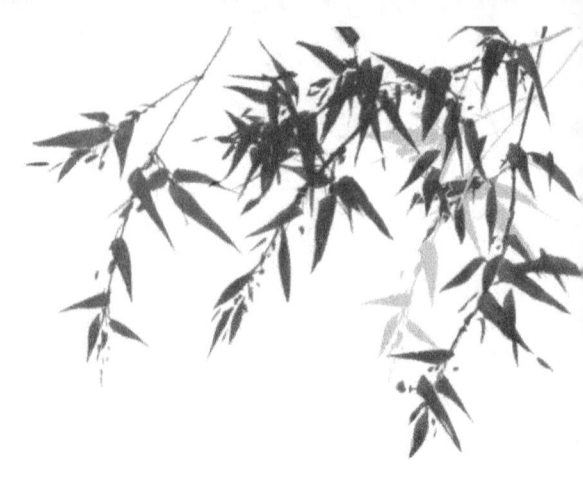

The difference between good and evil is training.

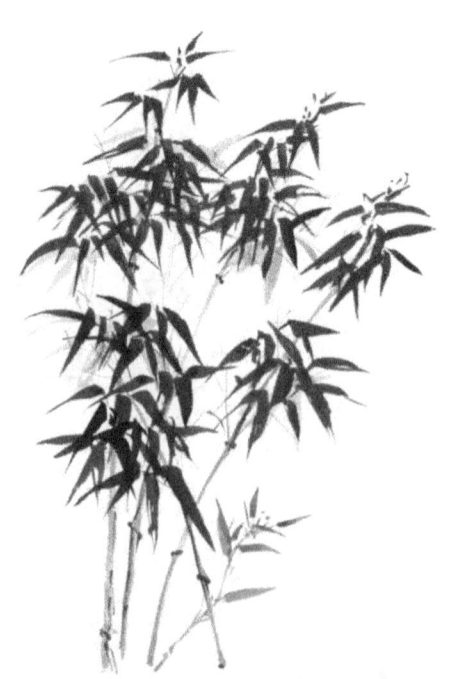

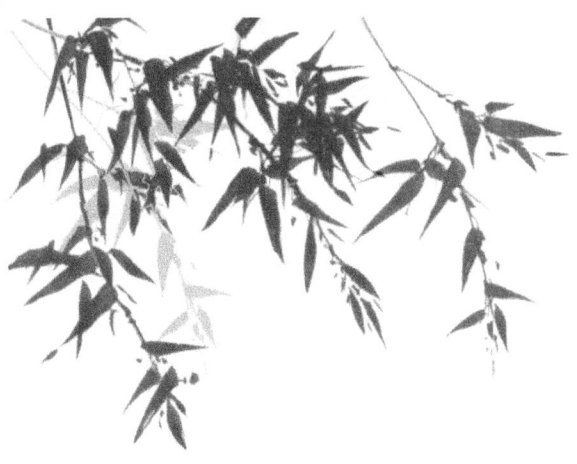

One lie focuses one to lie about the lie.

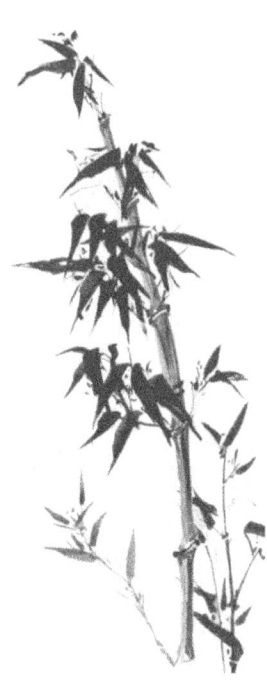

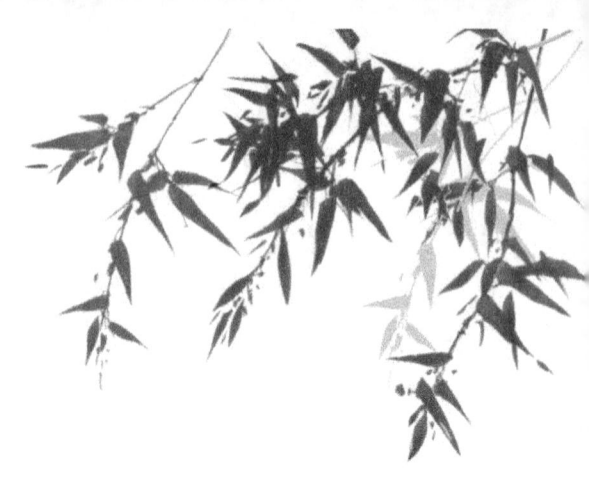

Sun out, Moon down
Leaves drop with no care.
Jolly times upon us.

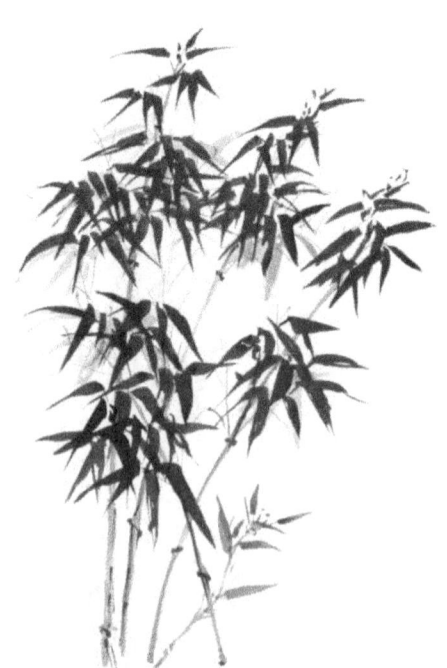

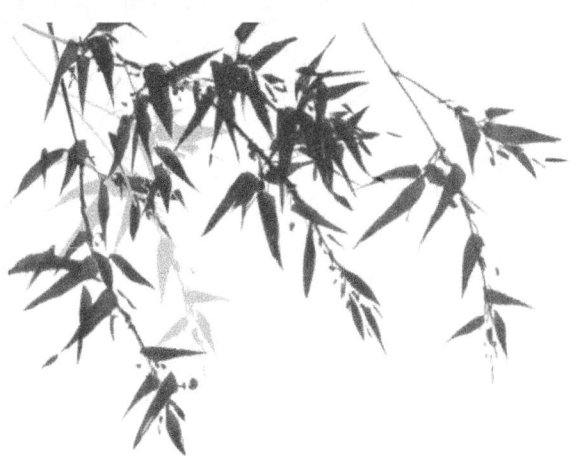

The season's change for us.
Mistletoes and sunflowers become one.
Life is but a midsummer dream.

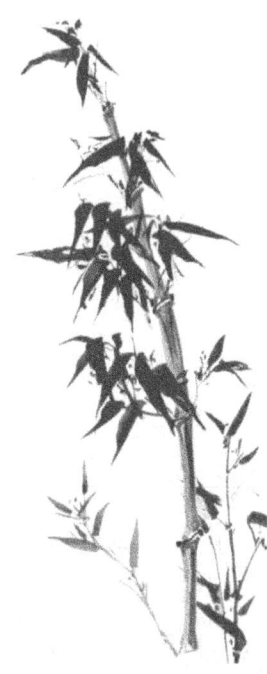

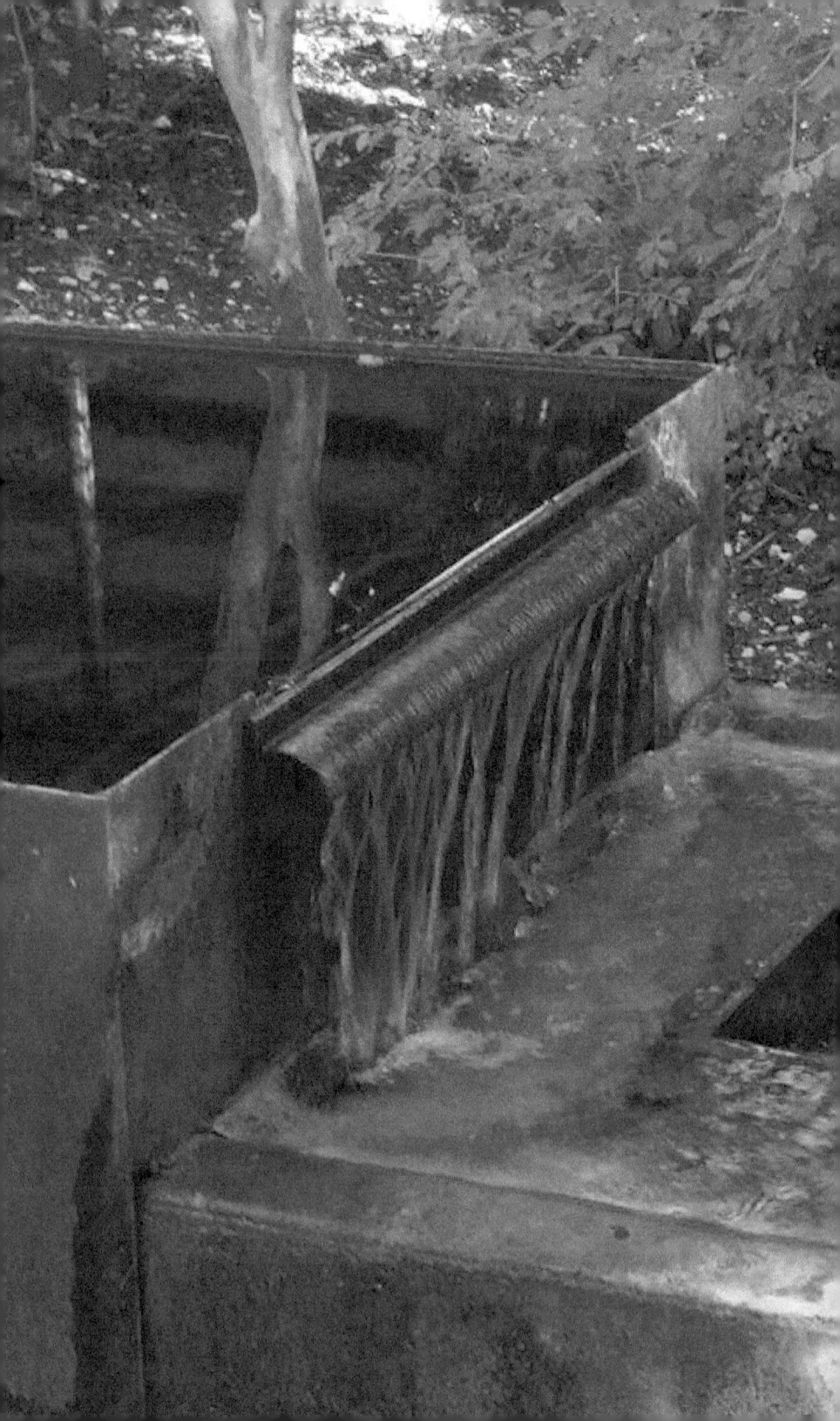

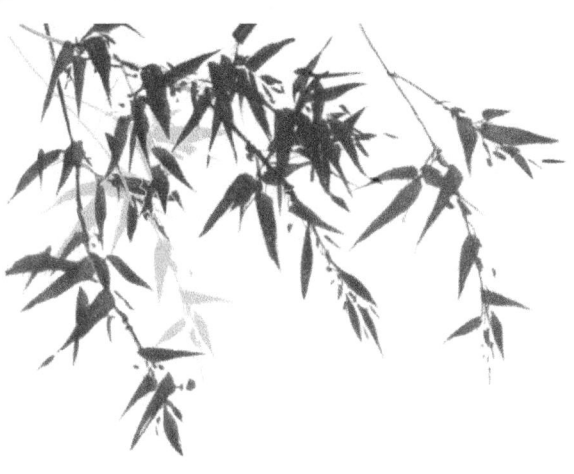

Warriors train for everyday battles.
Losing is not an option.

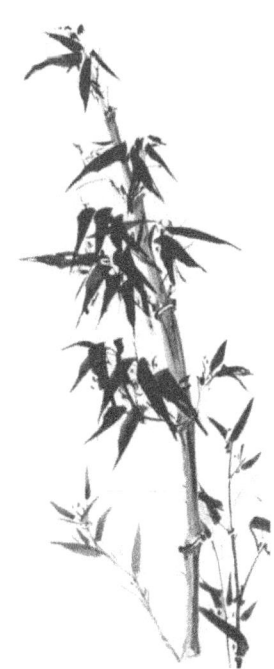

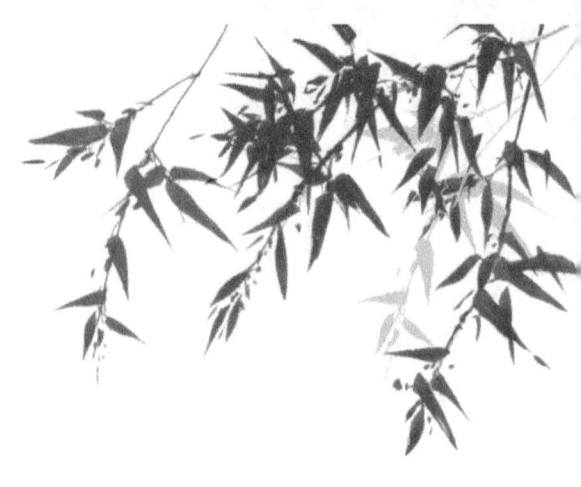

Don't be fooled by the fool inside yourself.
As the fool takes over, the leaves of life turn brown.

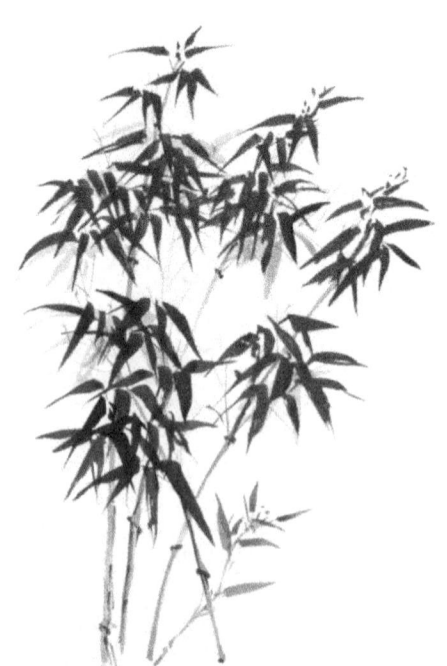

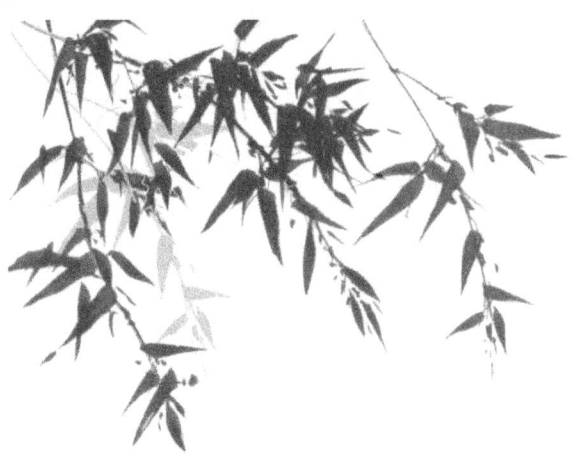

Not knowing is the worst,
was repeated by the person at the end of the line.

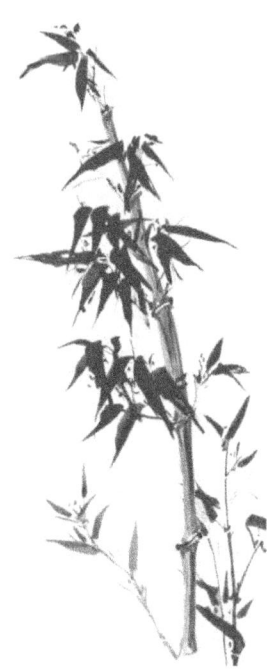

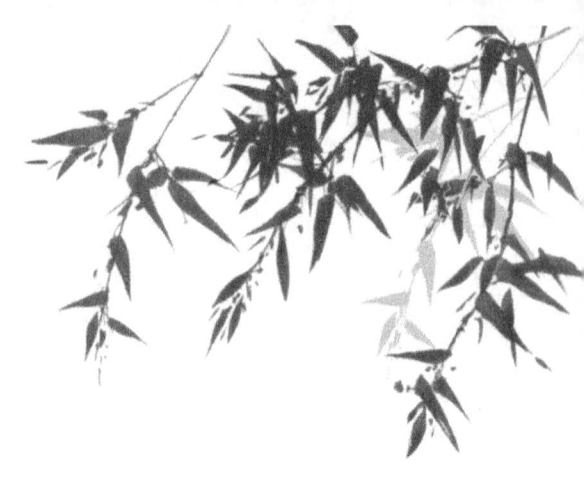

The energy of life is more powerful
than the mighty ant,
yet both are the same.

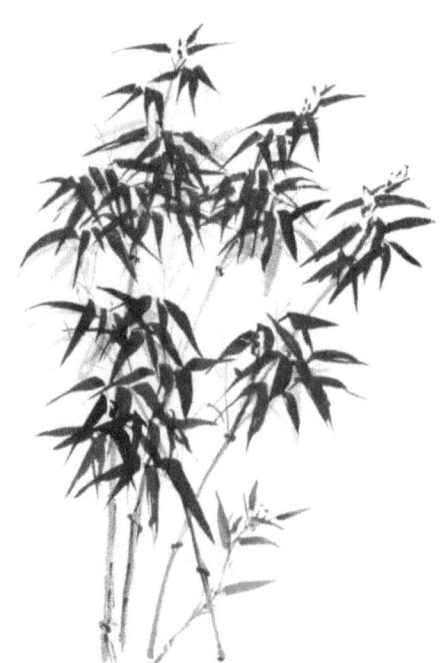

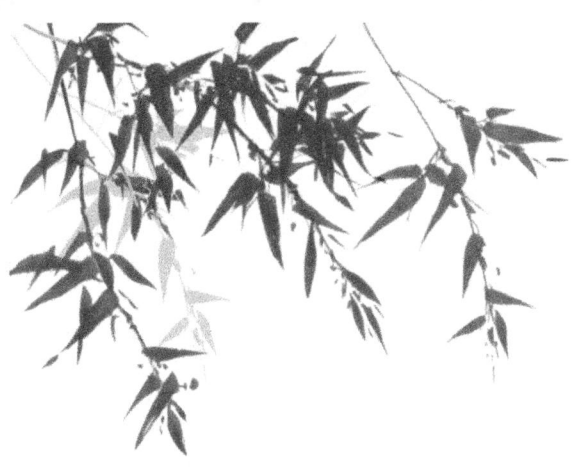

What is life? Who is life?
Live life and don't fold your hand.
Expand your vision and enjoy life.

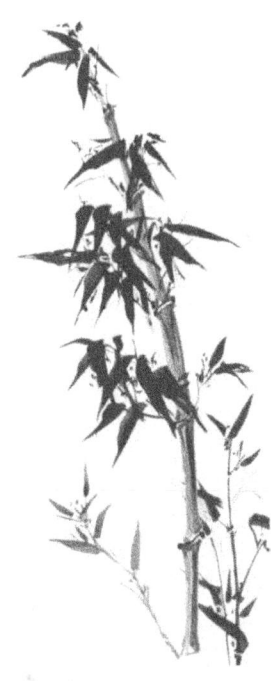

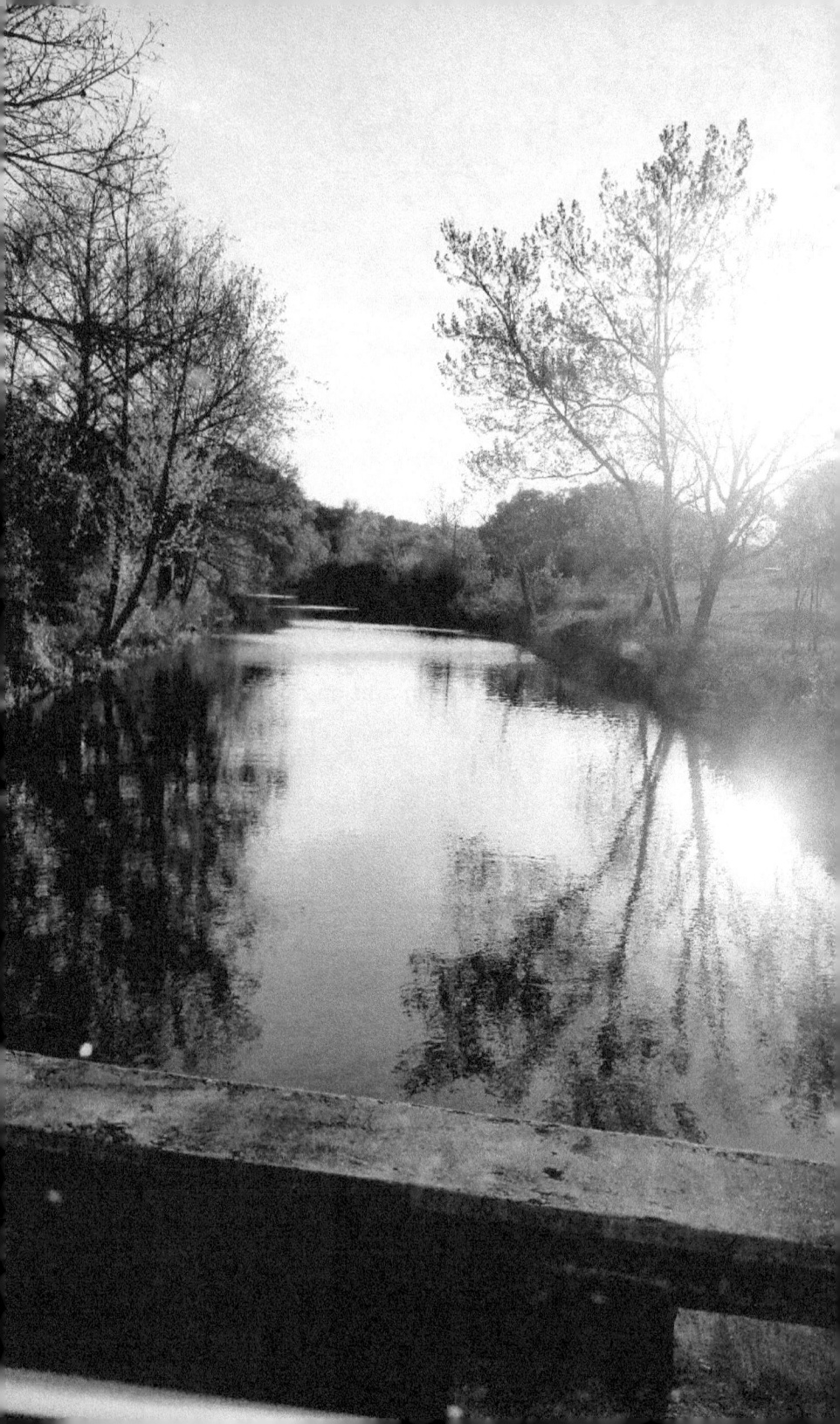

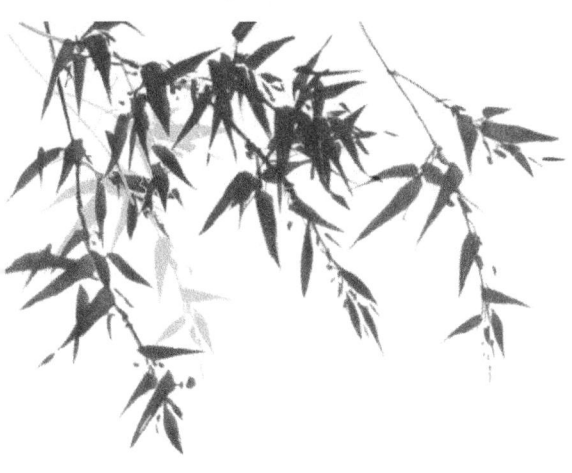

A tree is an extension
of the earth's entire beauty.

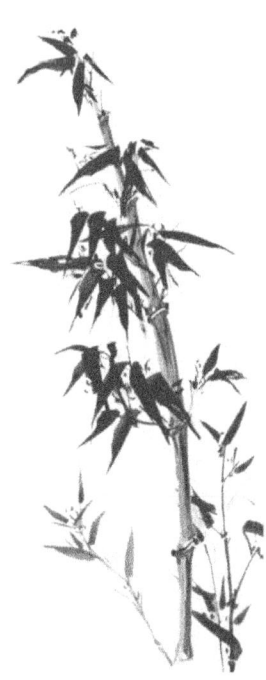

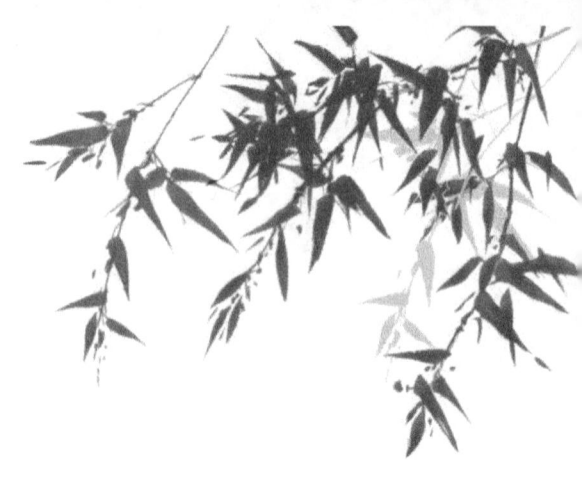

Family is more important than money,
money is more important than death,
which is more important,
the fool or the king?

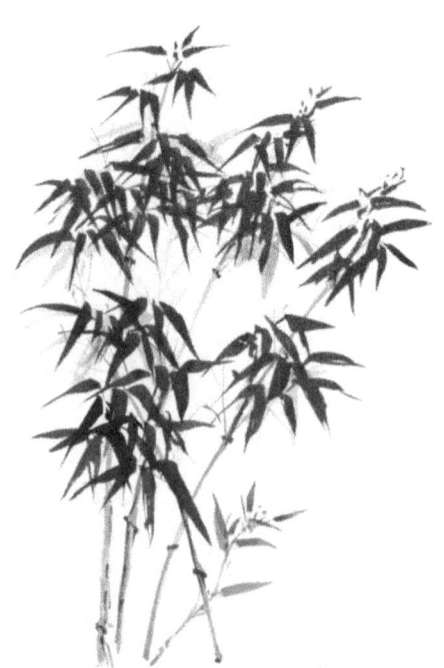

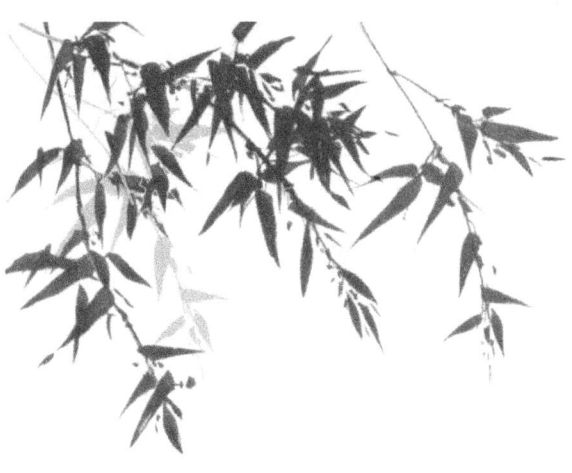

As the sun sets, don't talk.
Embrace and live in the moment.

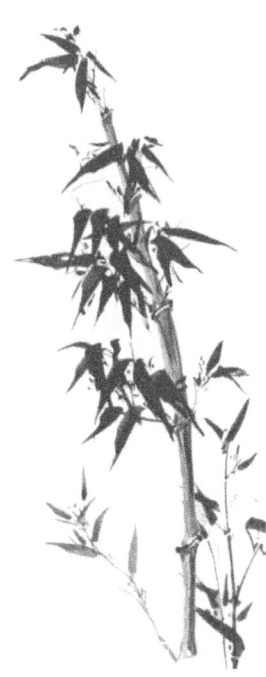

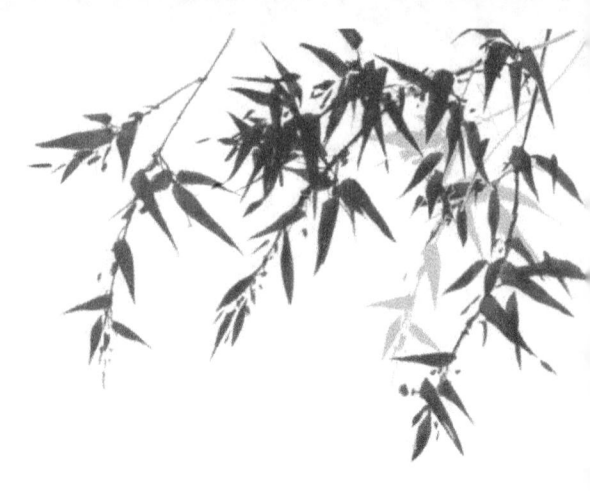

Don't look at the water
if you not ready to work on self.

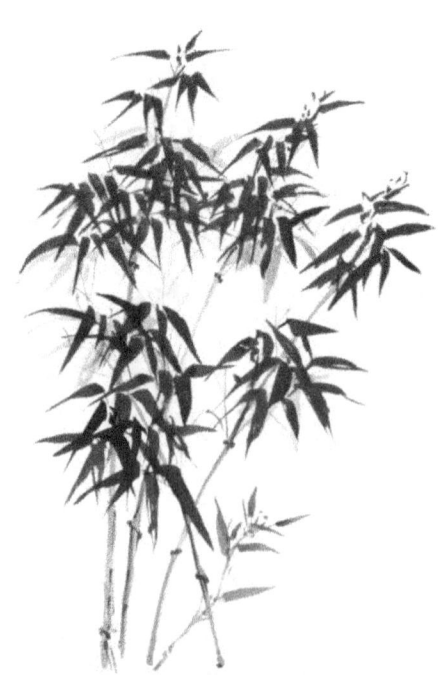

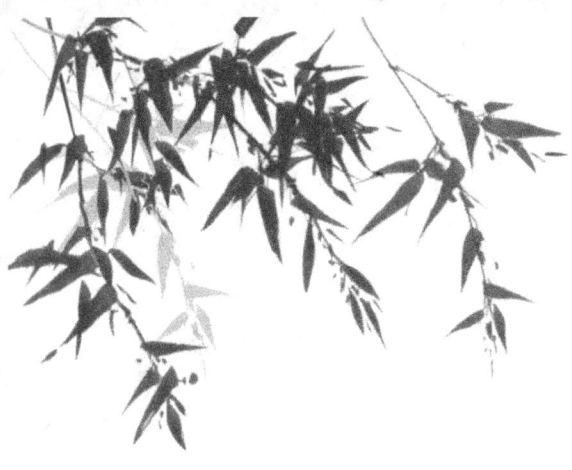

As I walk through life's path,
I often wonder, who has been here before?

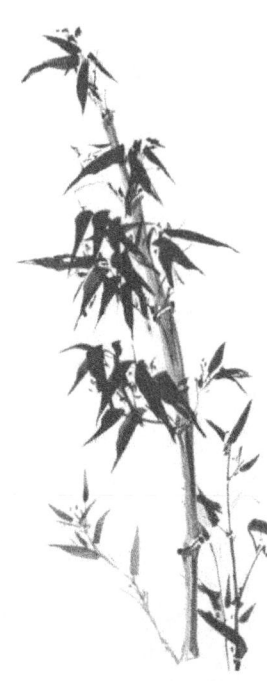

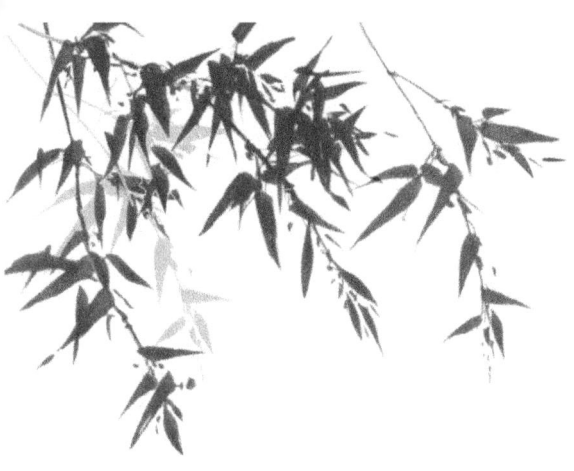

Life is like a dragonfly path.
The wind of seasons changes one destination.

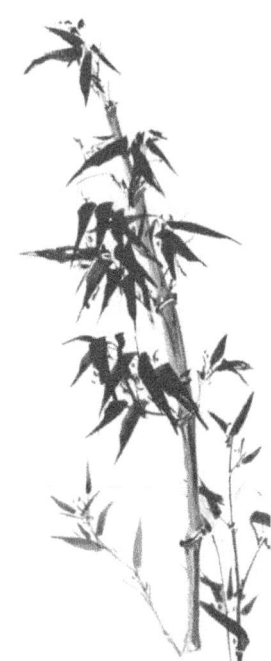

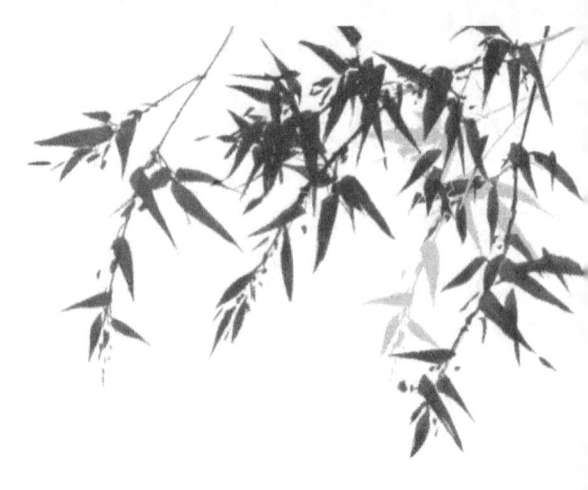

Music and silence
are extremely important in one's life.

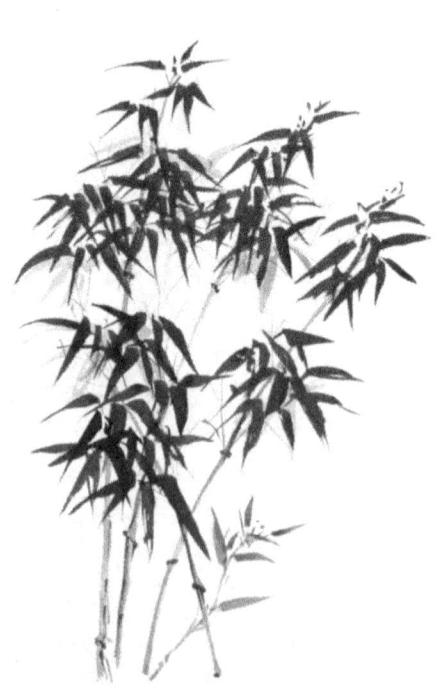

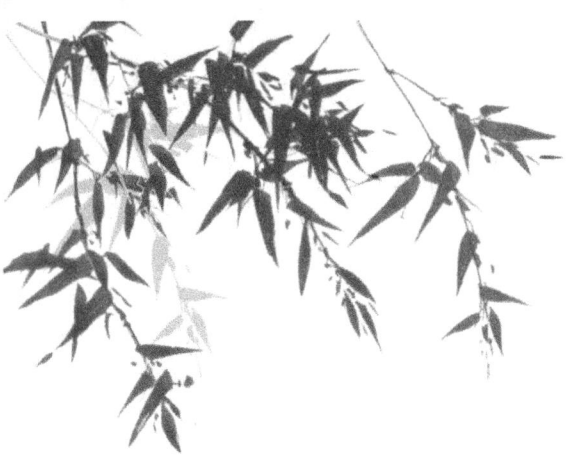

If a good person meditates,
they will grow to become a great person with time.

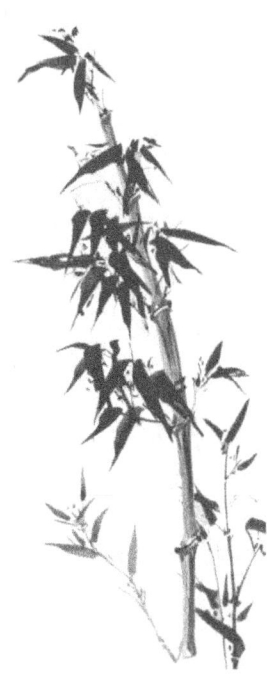

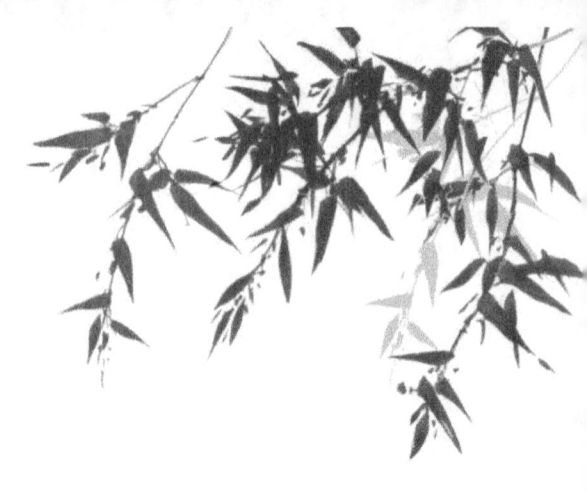

If life was too easy,
Man would not have invented ladders.

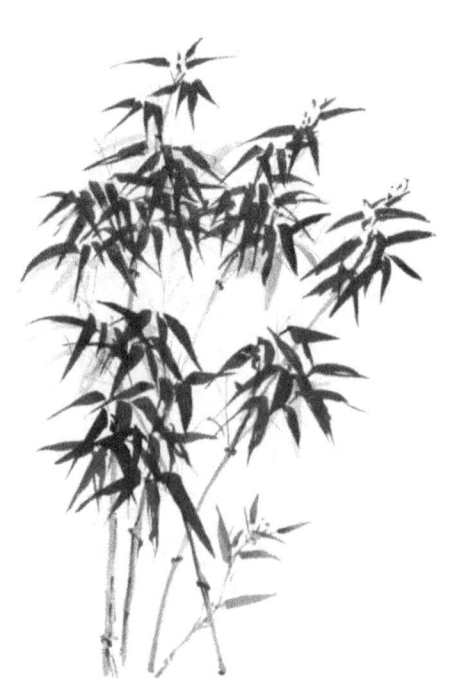

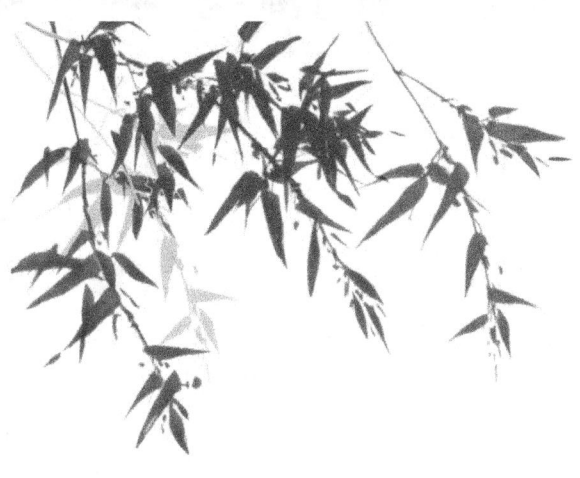

Don't give up or turn away,
move forward with the same attitude
that got you to that point.

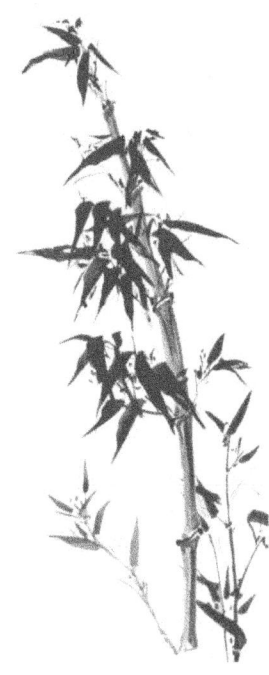

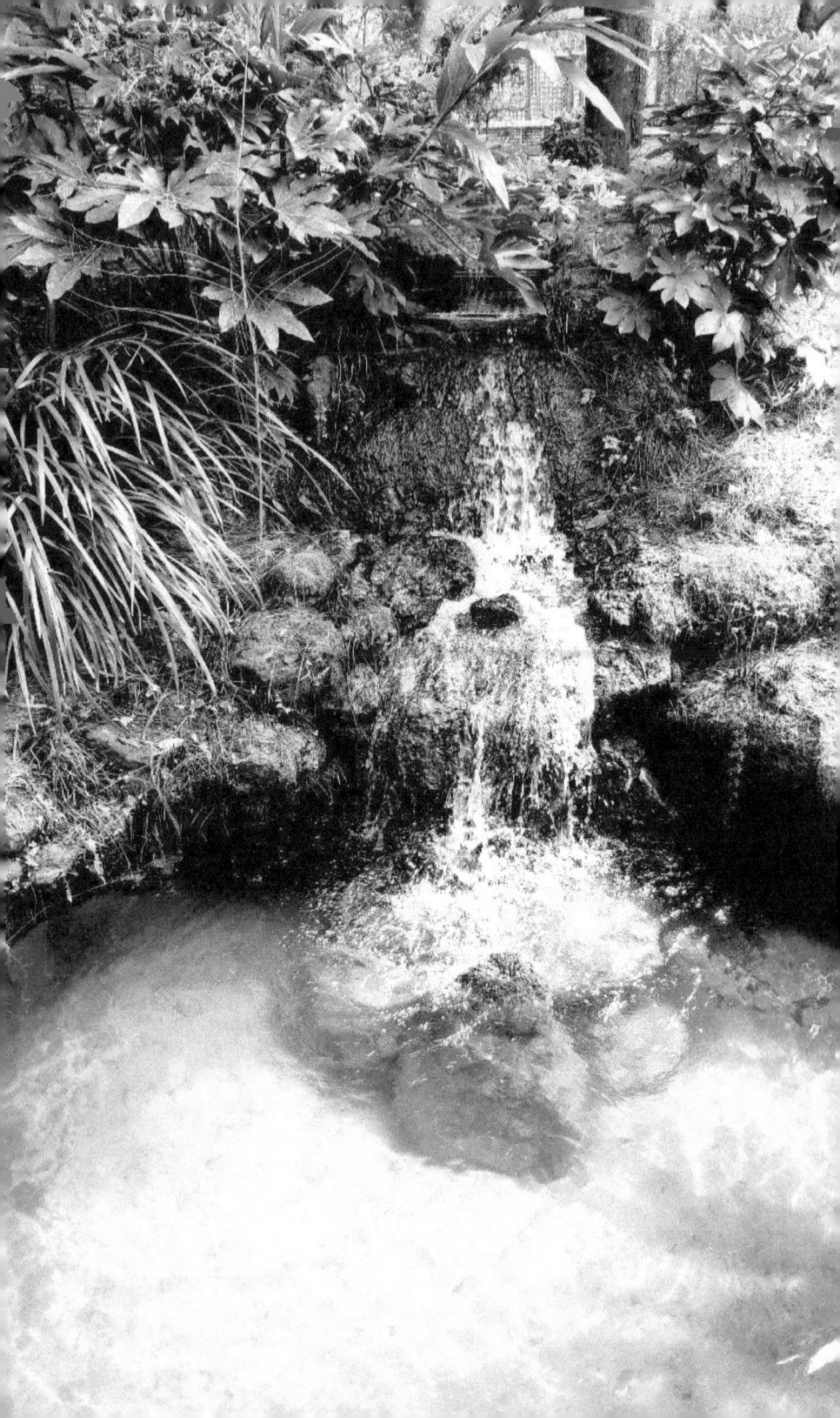

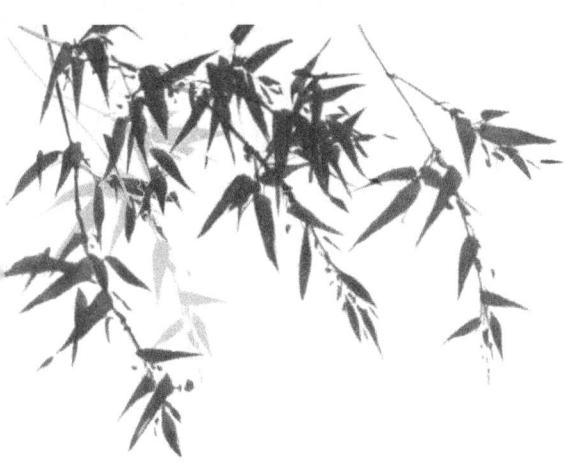

There are those that complain
about grains of sand.
Then there are those
that love grains of sand between their toes.

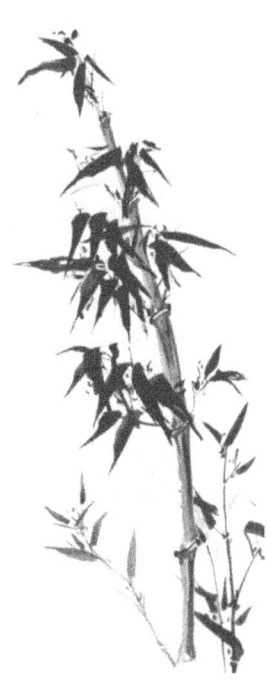

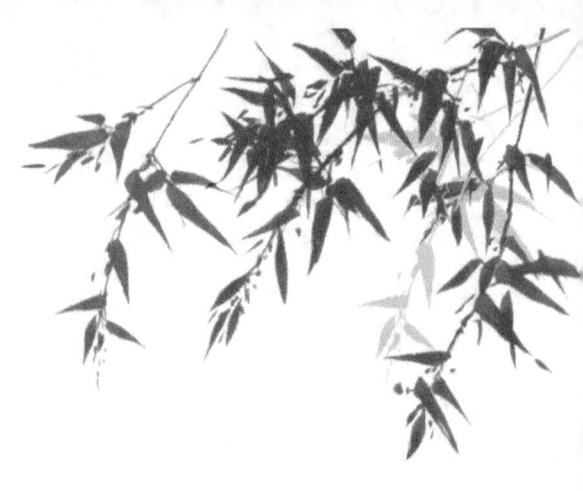

The three things that make humans better.
Say the truth
See the truth
Be the truth

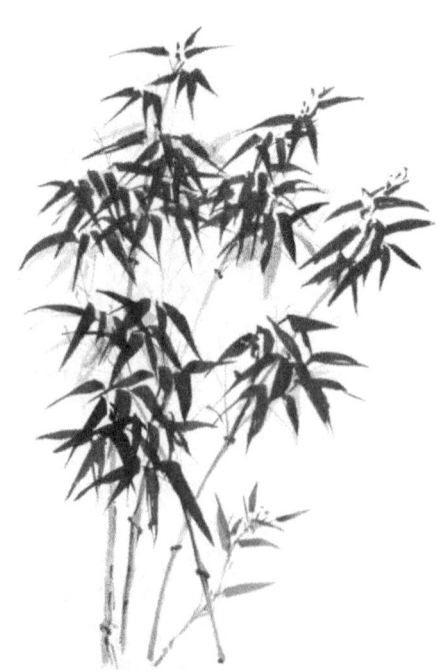

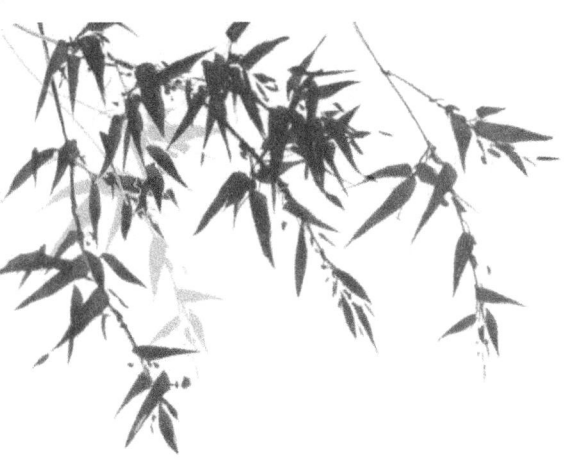

There is no greater stranger
than one who does not know self.

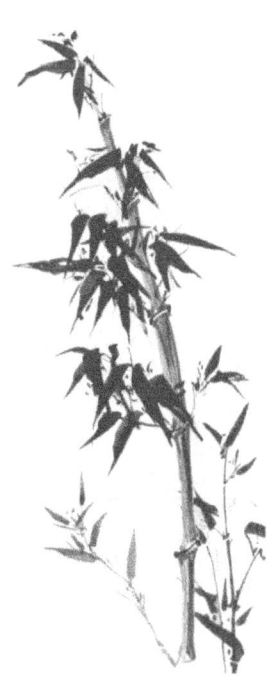

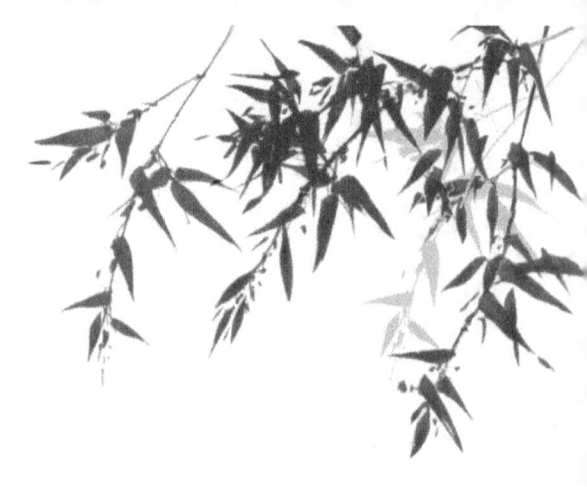

Treat today as if it's the greatest day in your life.
Then watch the changes in your life.

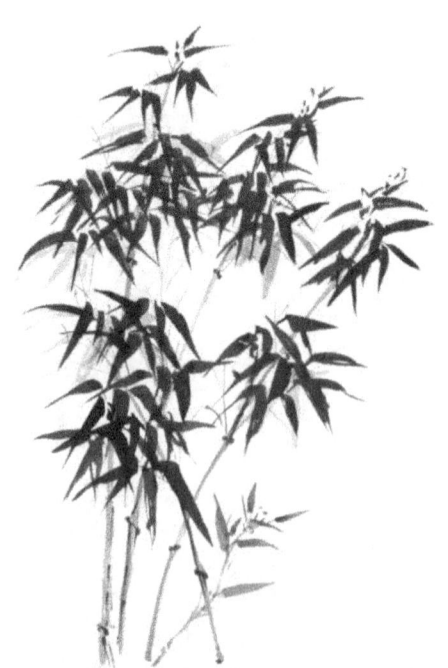

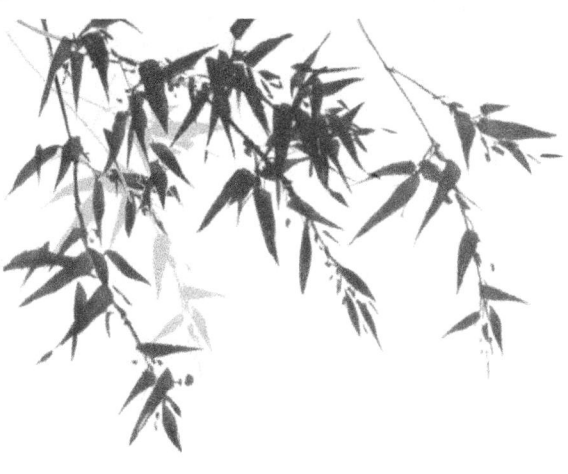

By dawn's early light, who took my cookies and milk? Look to the west, south, east and north. But the answer may be within self.

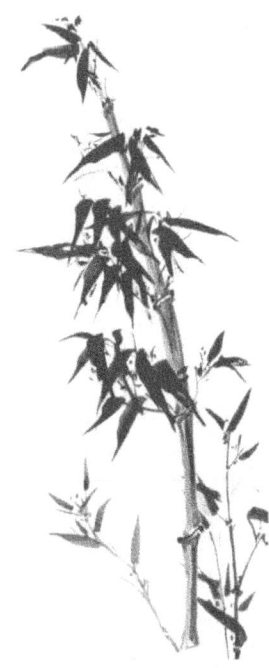

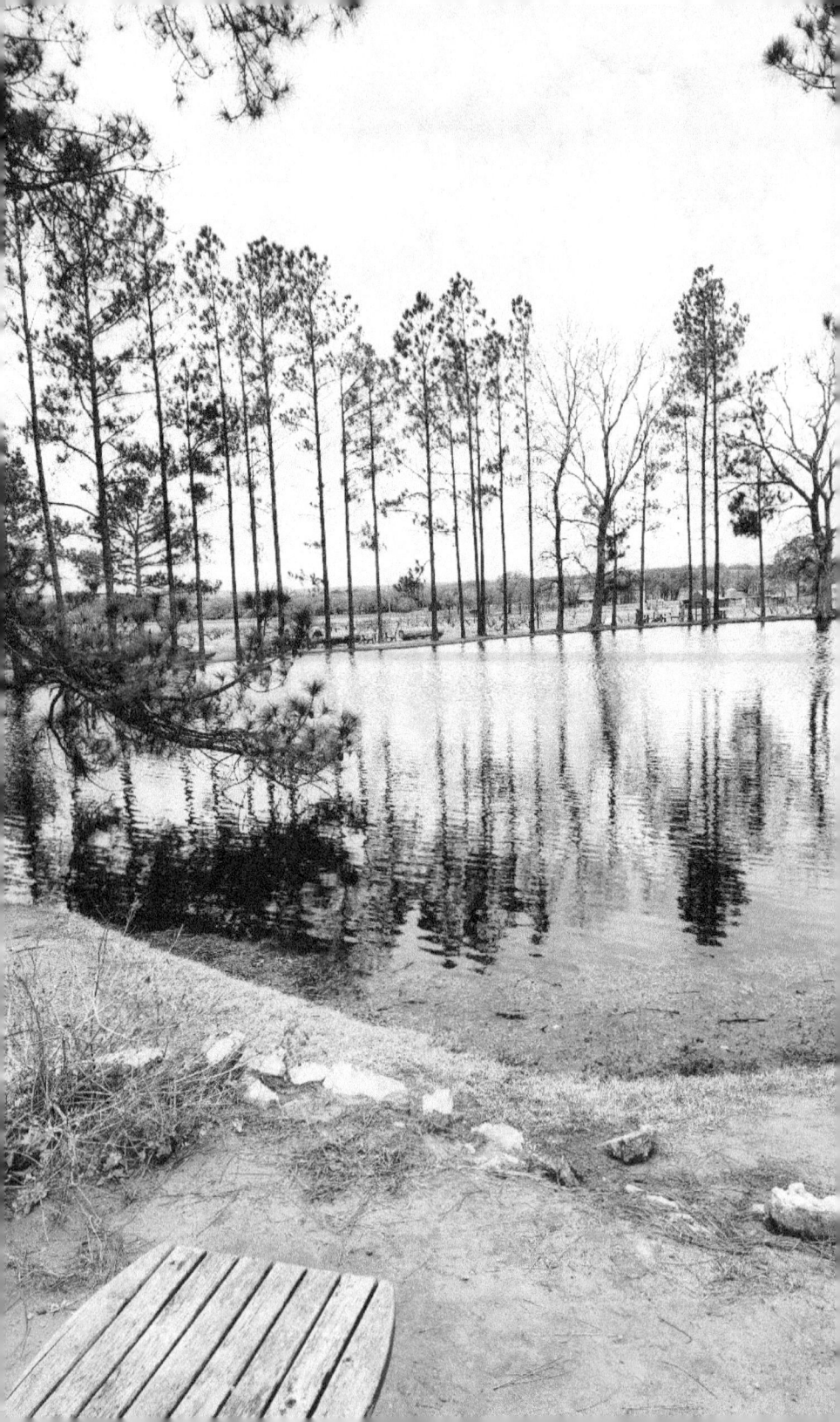

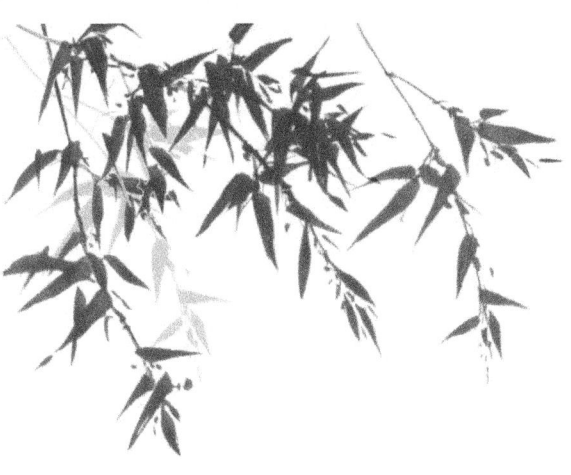

To enjoy life and all its beauty is fantastic.
People that don't enjoy life
must feel like a bug on a windshield.

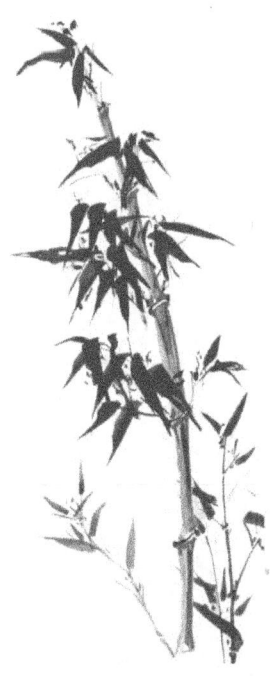

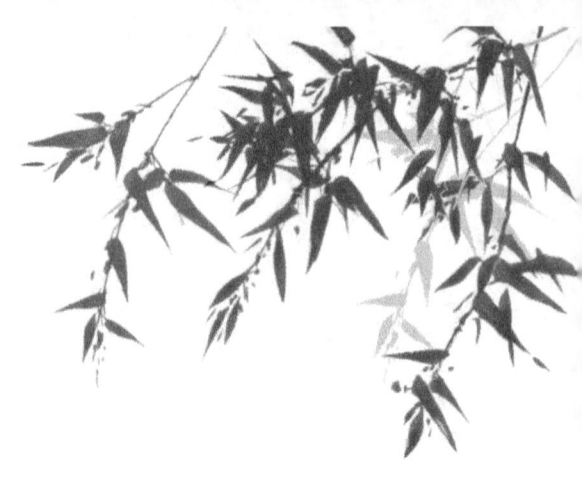

Any wall can be overcome.
Any lake can be overcome.
Any distance can be overcome.
Don't be the fool that thinks
nothing can be overcome.

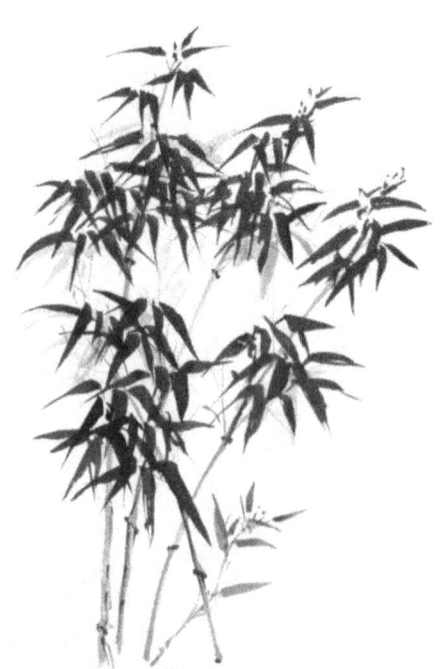

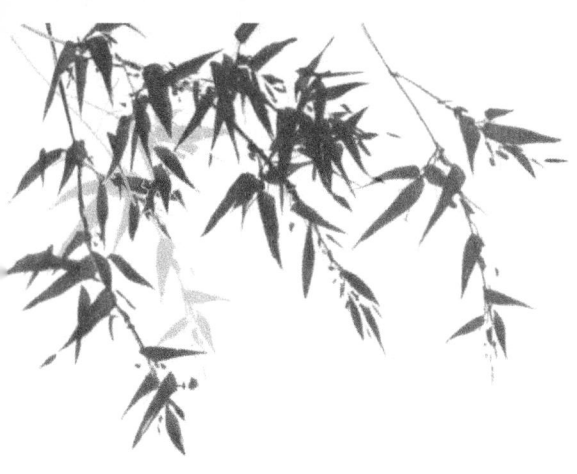

The past is the past. Learn and move on.

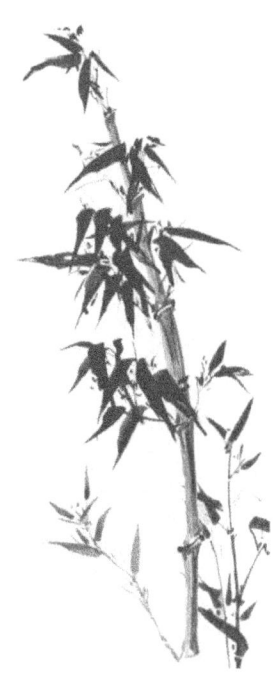

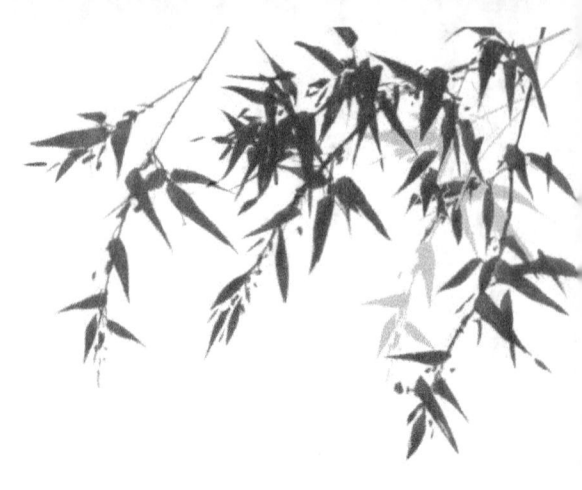

The butterfly was created
by the same that created concrete.

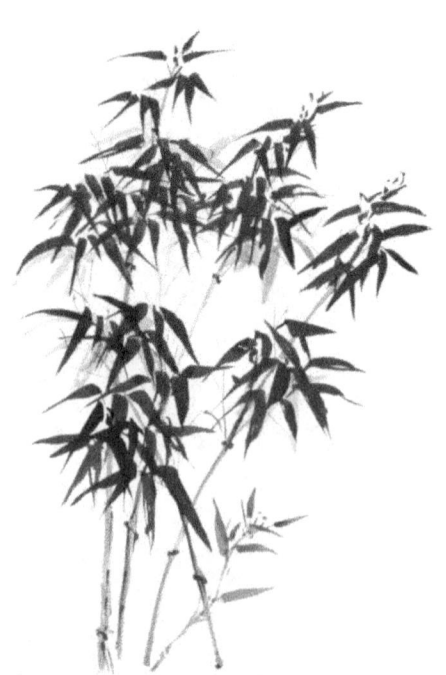

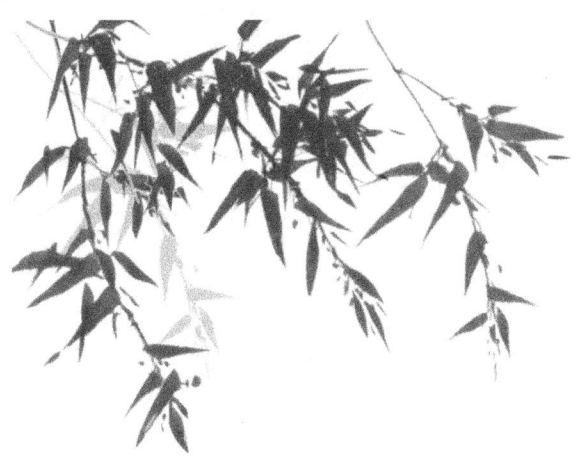

Which is more important?
The cart or the horse?

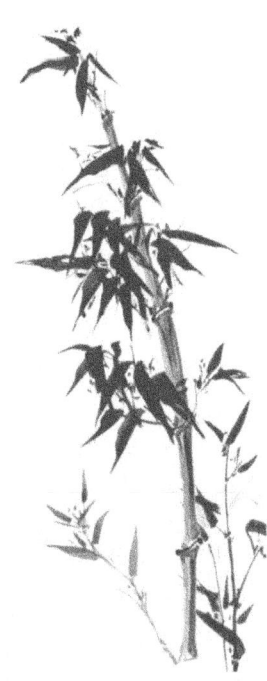

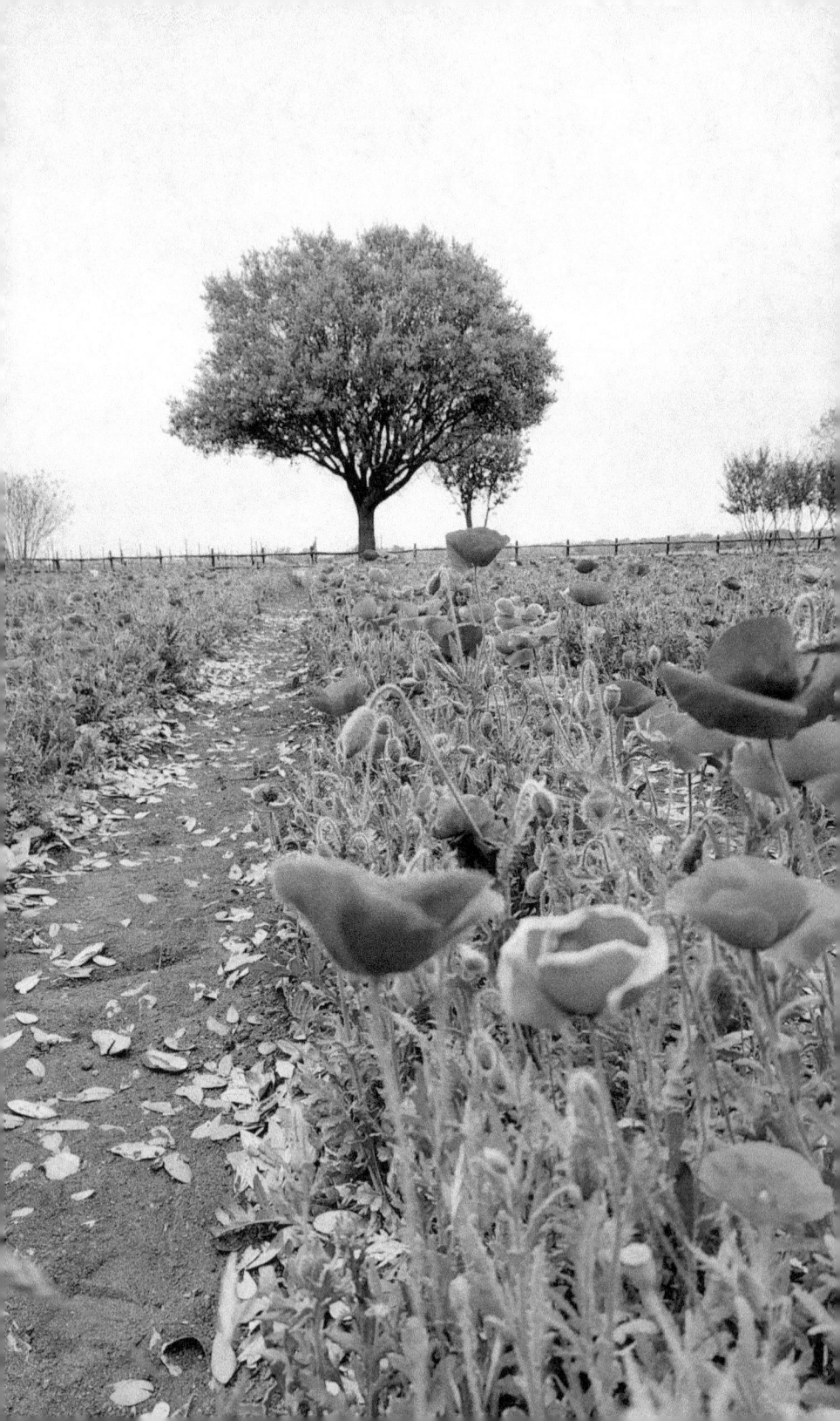

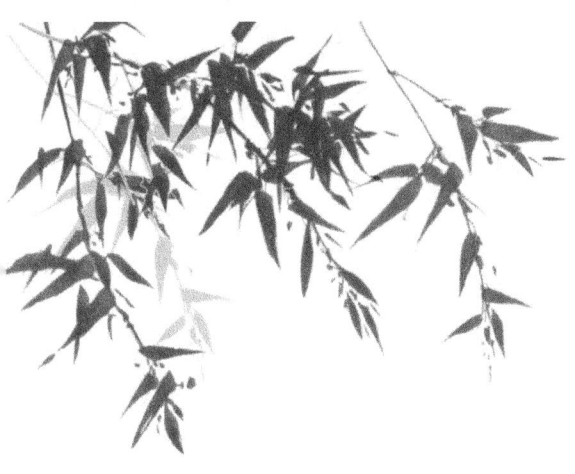

Everything in this world is alive.
Knowing this is a good start.

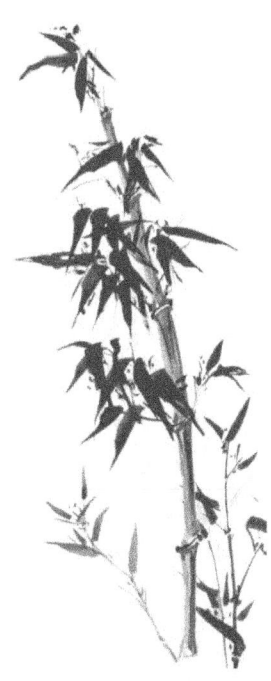

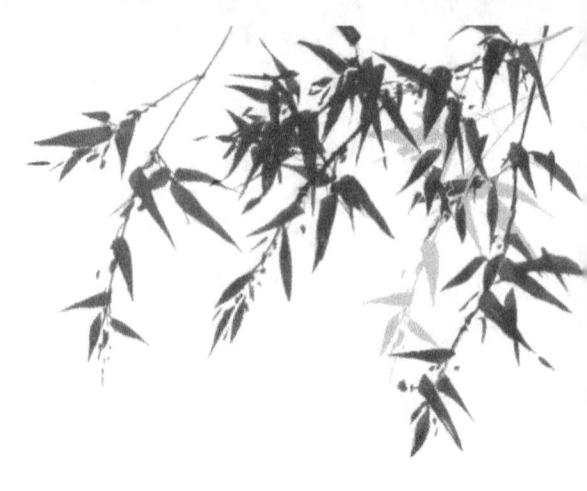

Everyday there is a lesson to be learned.

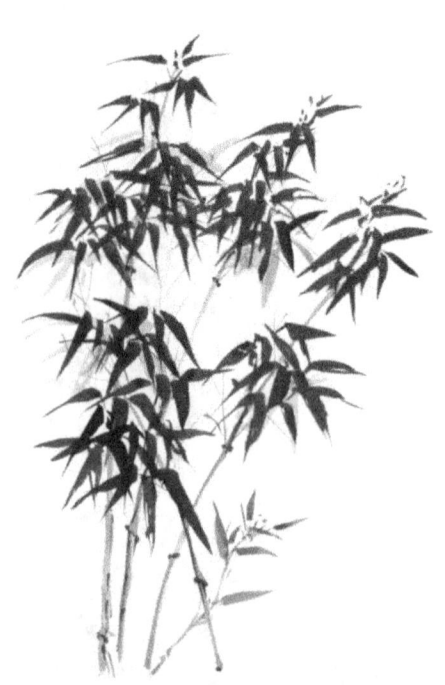

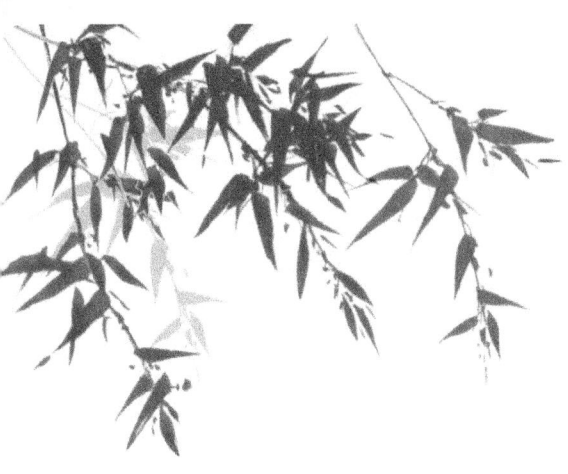

A person without creativity
is like a car without gears.

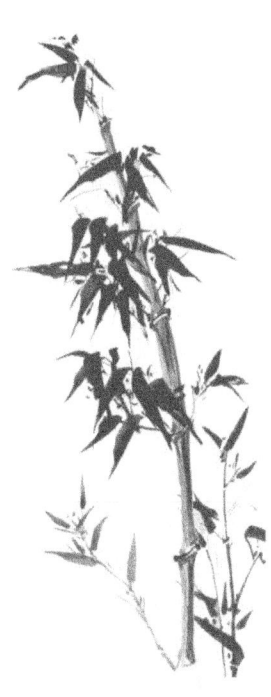

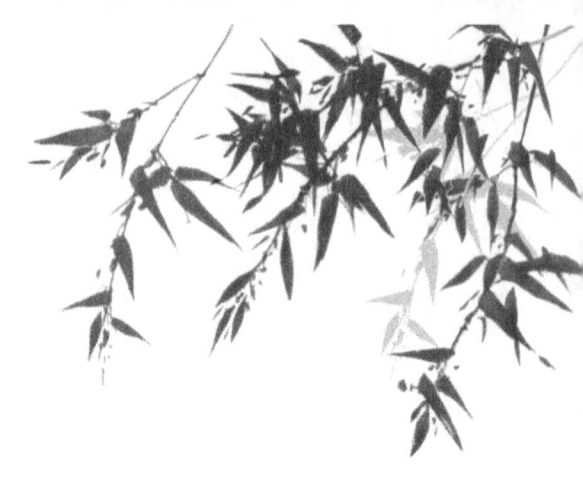

One must move like the wind
in order to cross a river.

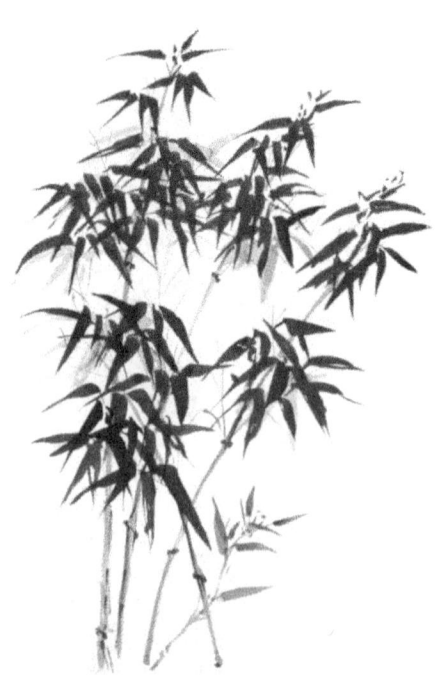

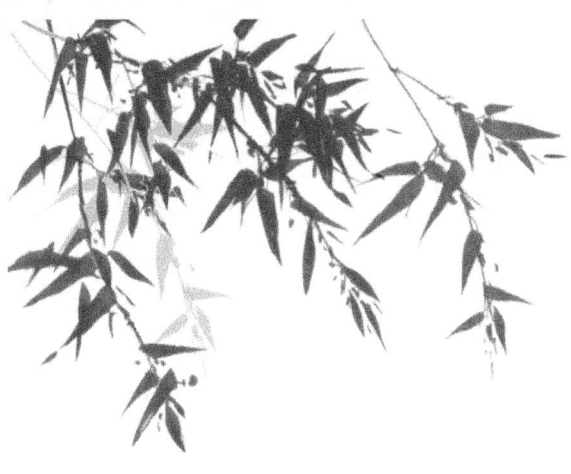

There are many noble working fields;
it's up to the worker to keep it noble.

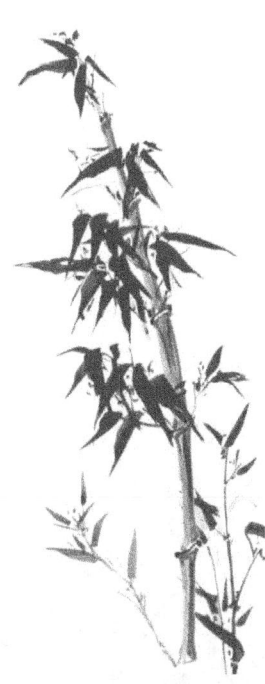

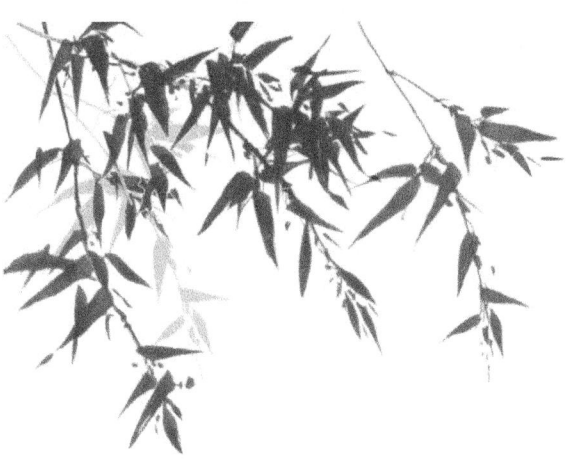

A sweet peach attracts all creatures.
The full moon mirrors the glass river.
Birds fly overhead with no discrimination.

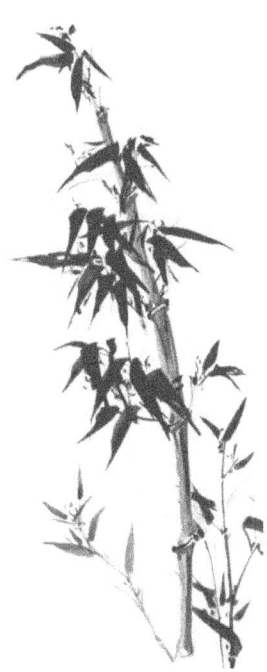

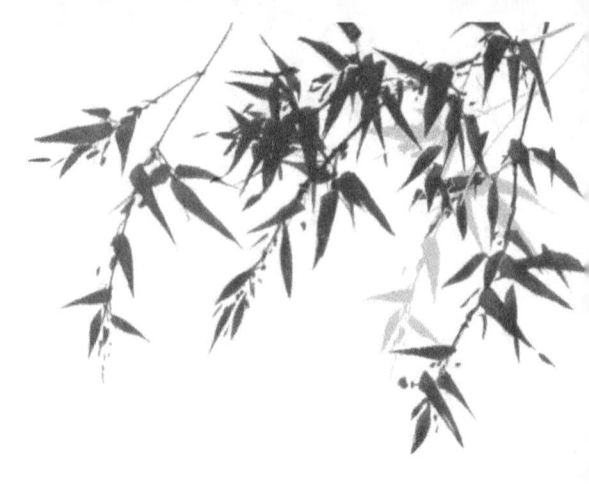

One's spirit can be felt by the world.

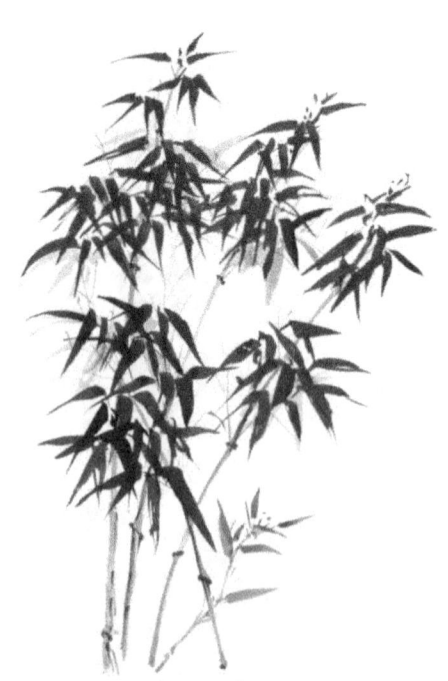

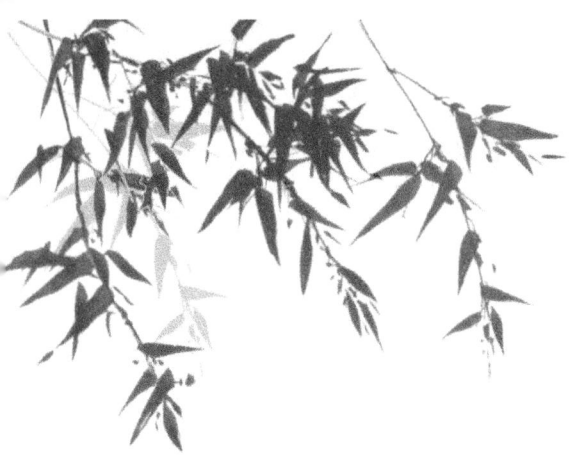

Joy is understood by those
that know how to have joy.

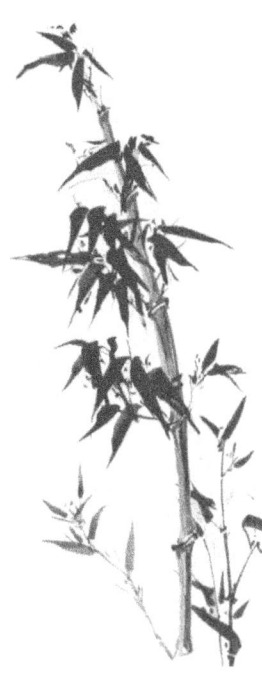

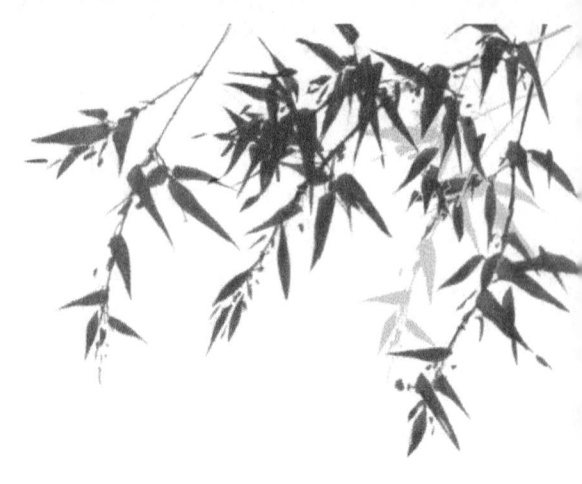

The yellow light comes into my soul
with the energy of a newborn.

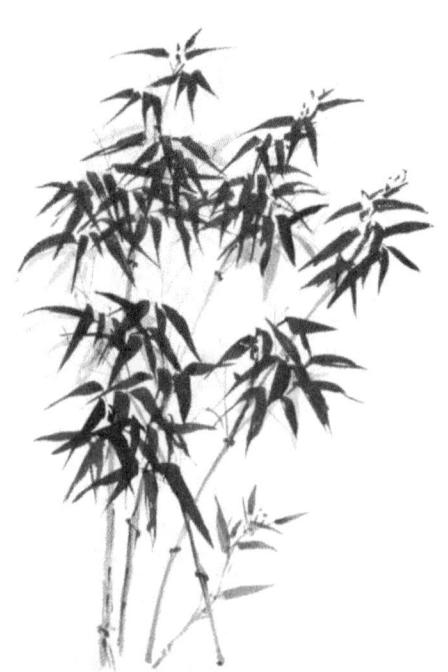

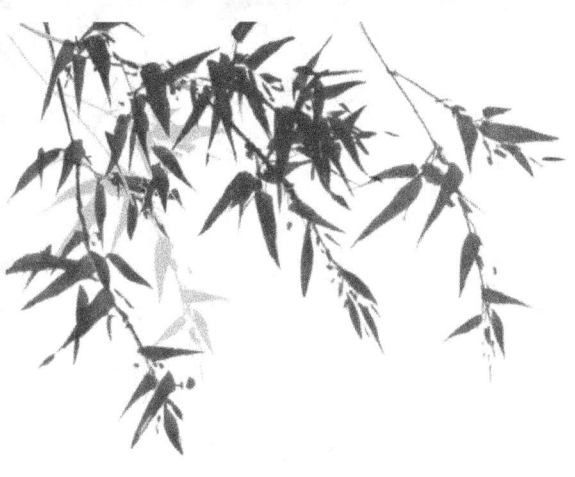

The sun and moon brought me
light, warmth, and magical influences
that words can't describe.

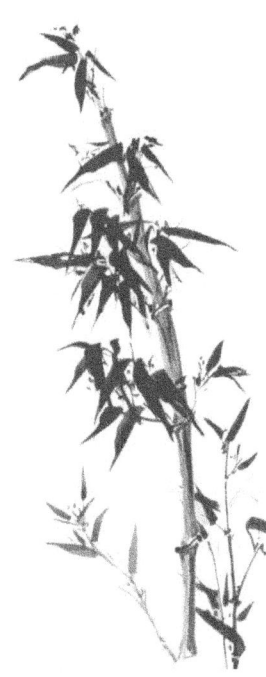

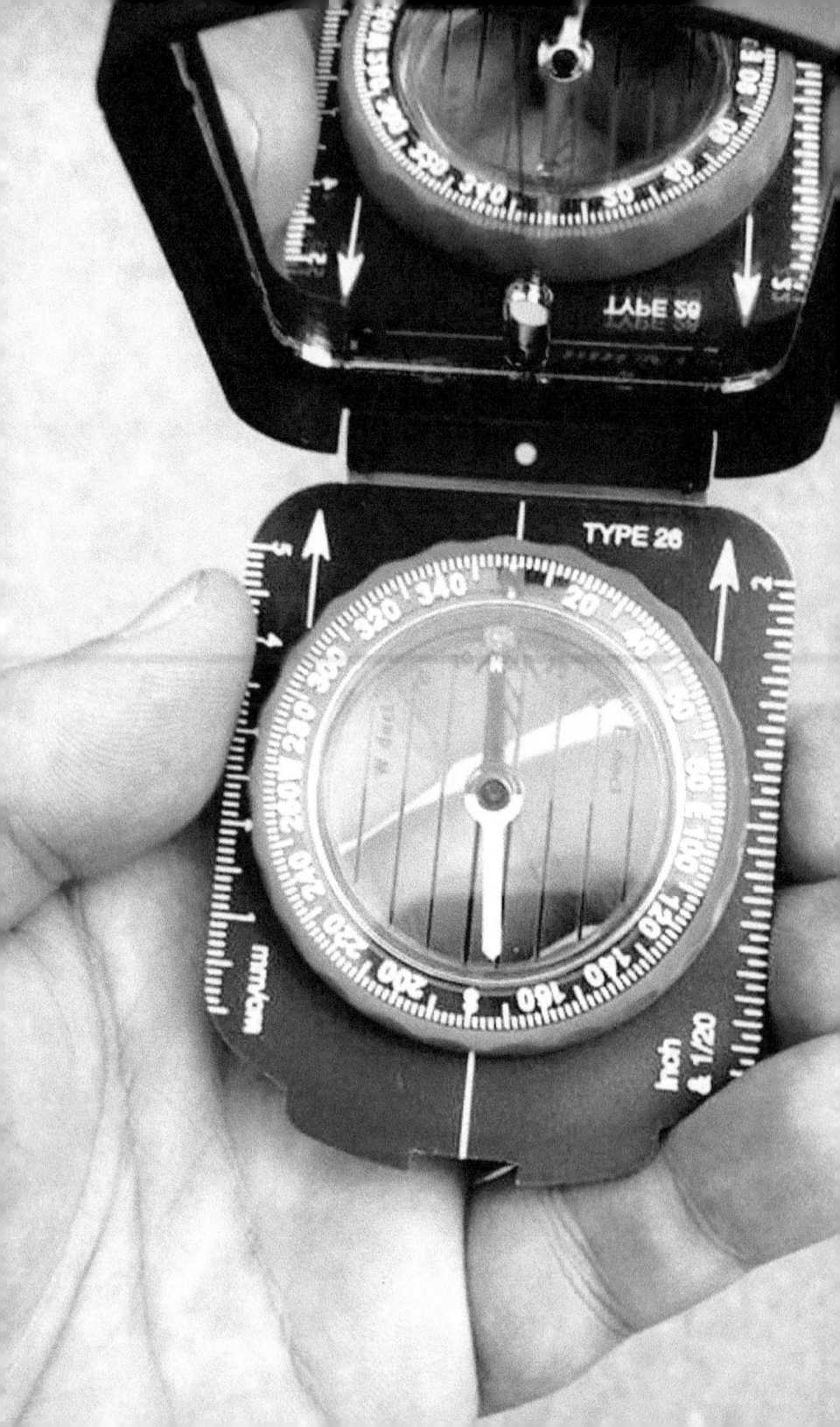

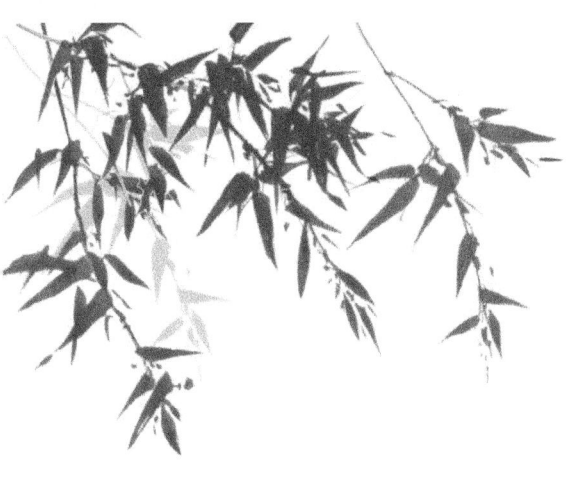

If we strip all possessions in life,
we can start a new life or death,
depending on one's compass.

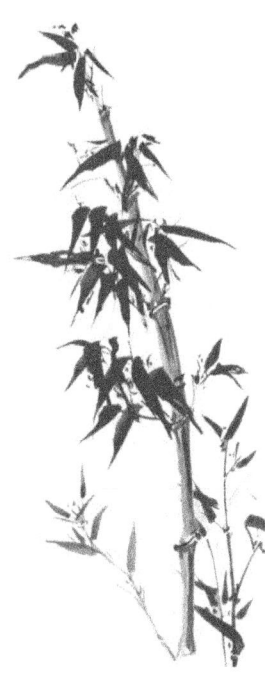

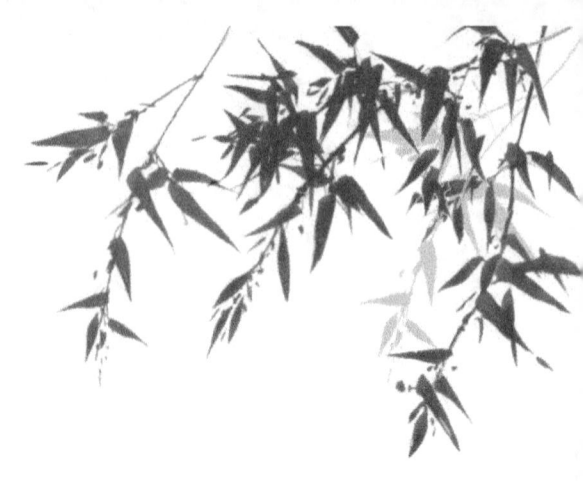

The music of our ancestors
molded and weaved the tapestry
of our limitless ambitions.

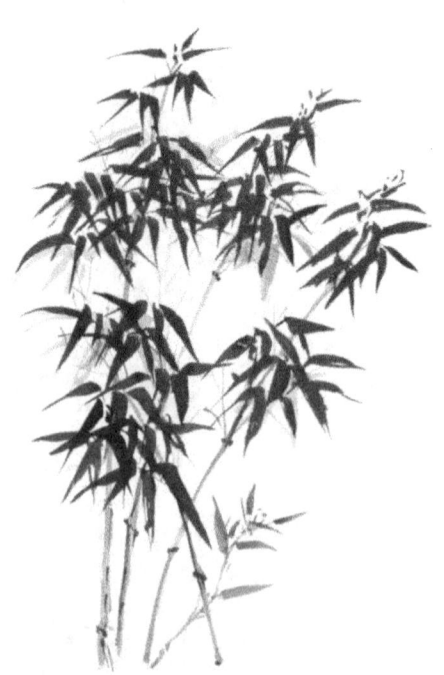

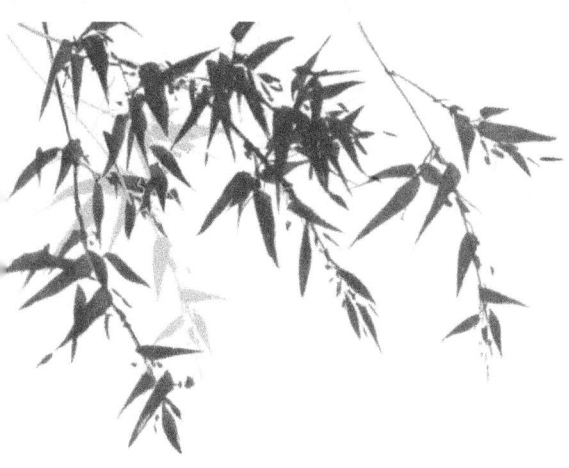

A child's mind can be the best detective.

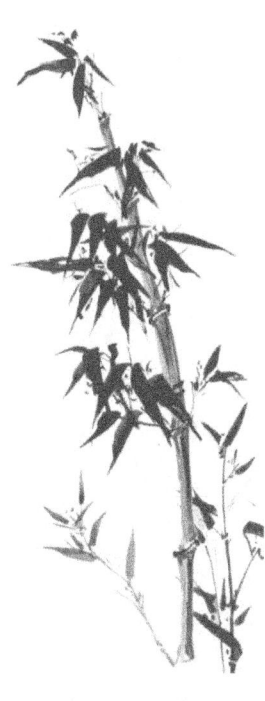

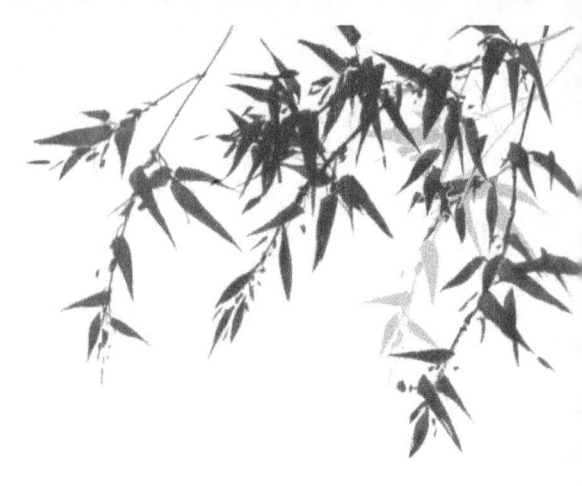

Remember, people are people,
no matter where they hang their hats.

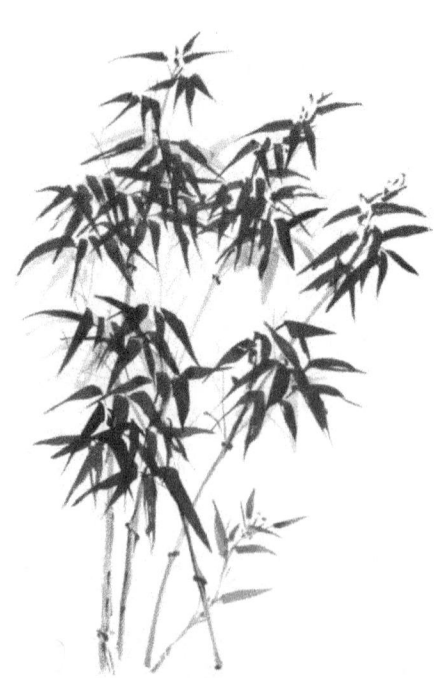

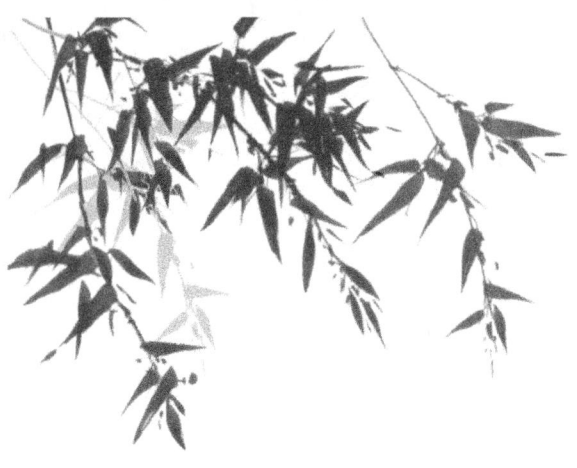

Love is only a word.

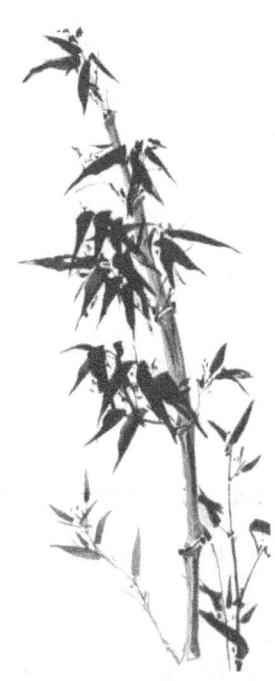

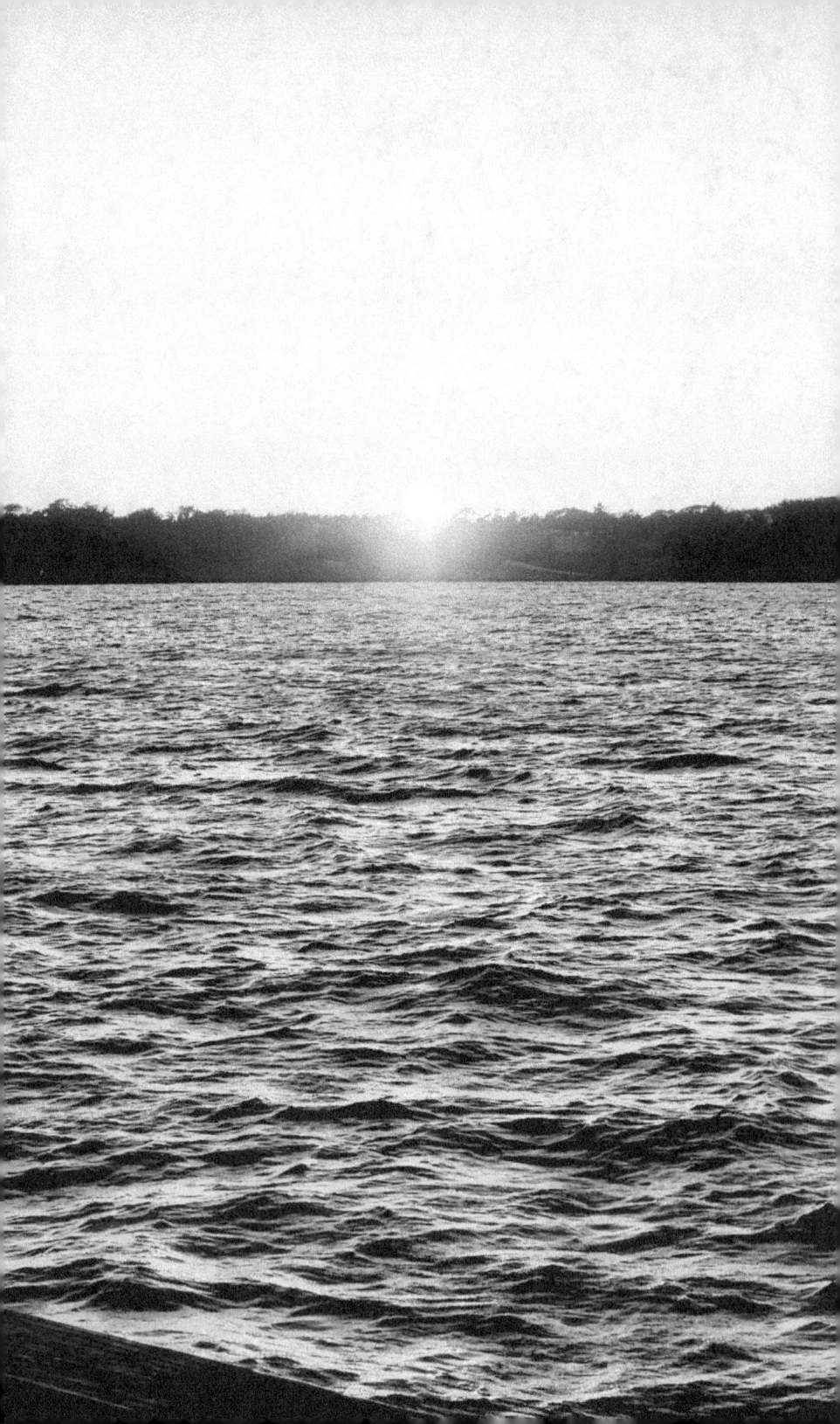

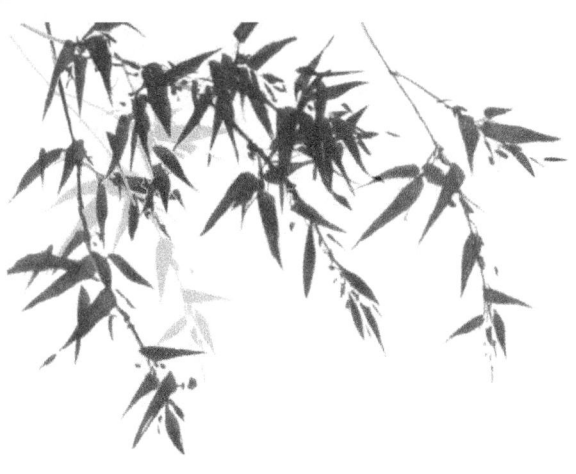

A quiet mind and heart,
listens to the world's silence.

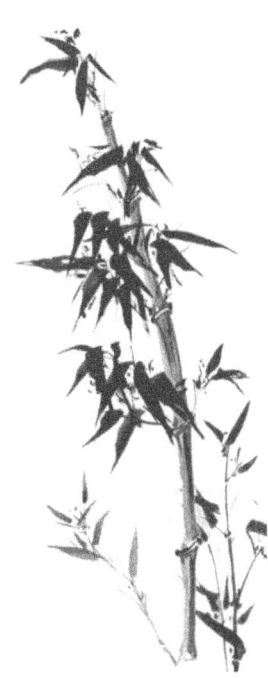

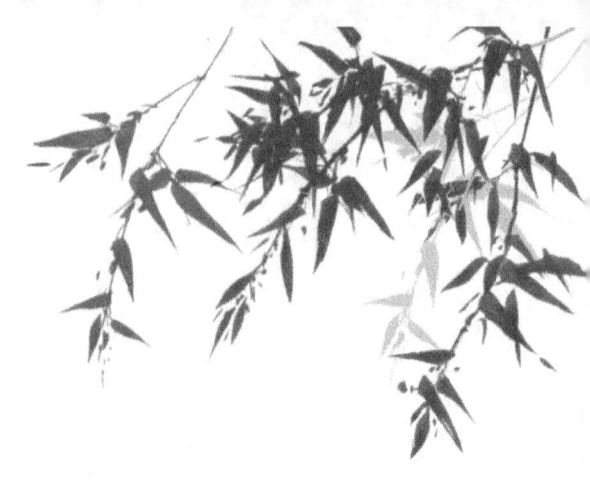

If one blindfolds self,
they have the potential of more vision
than a hawk on flight.

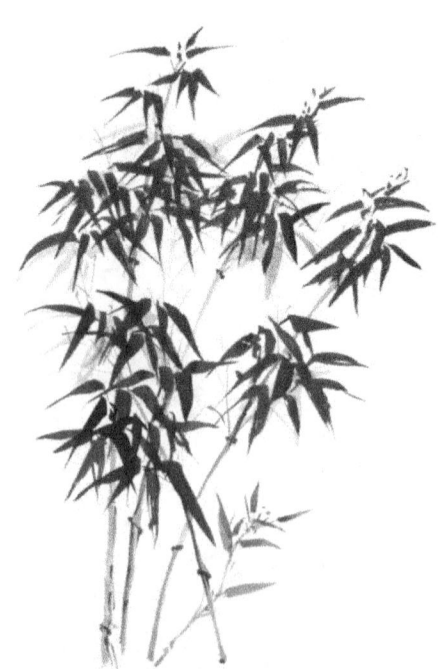

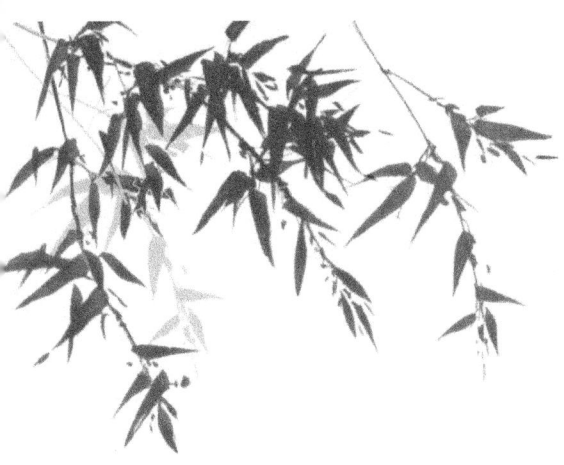

One who judges others is really judging self.

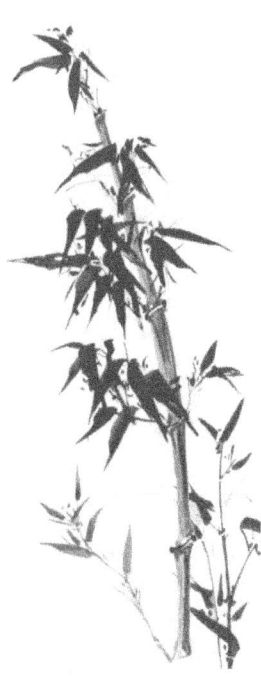

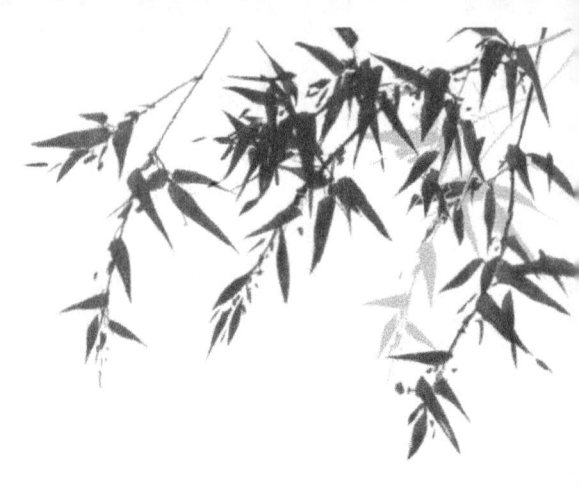

The sun rises and sets.
Humans' lives rise and set.

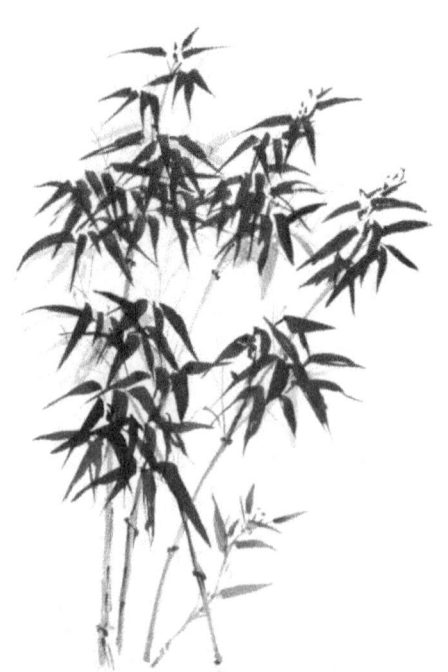

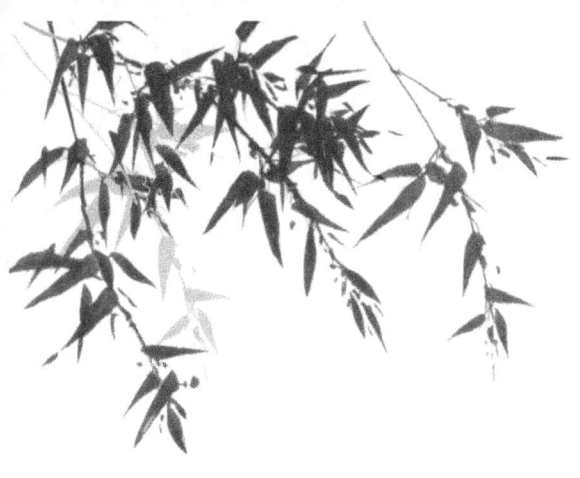

Blue is only a color.

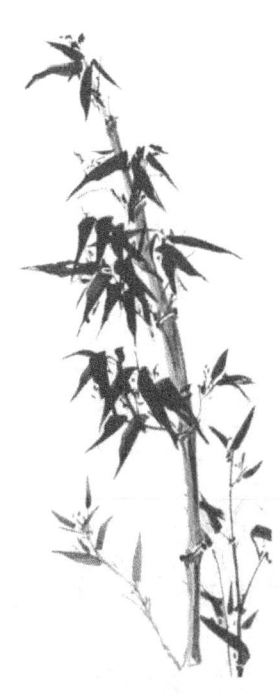

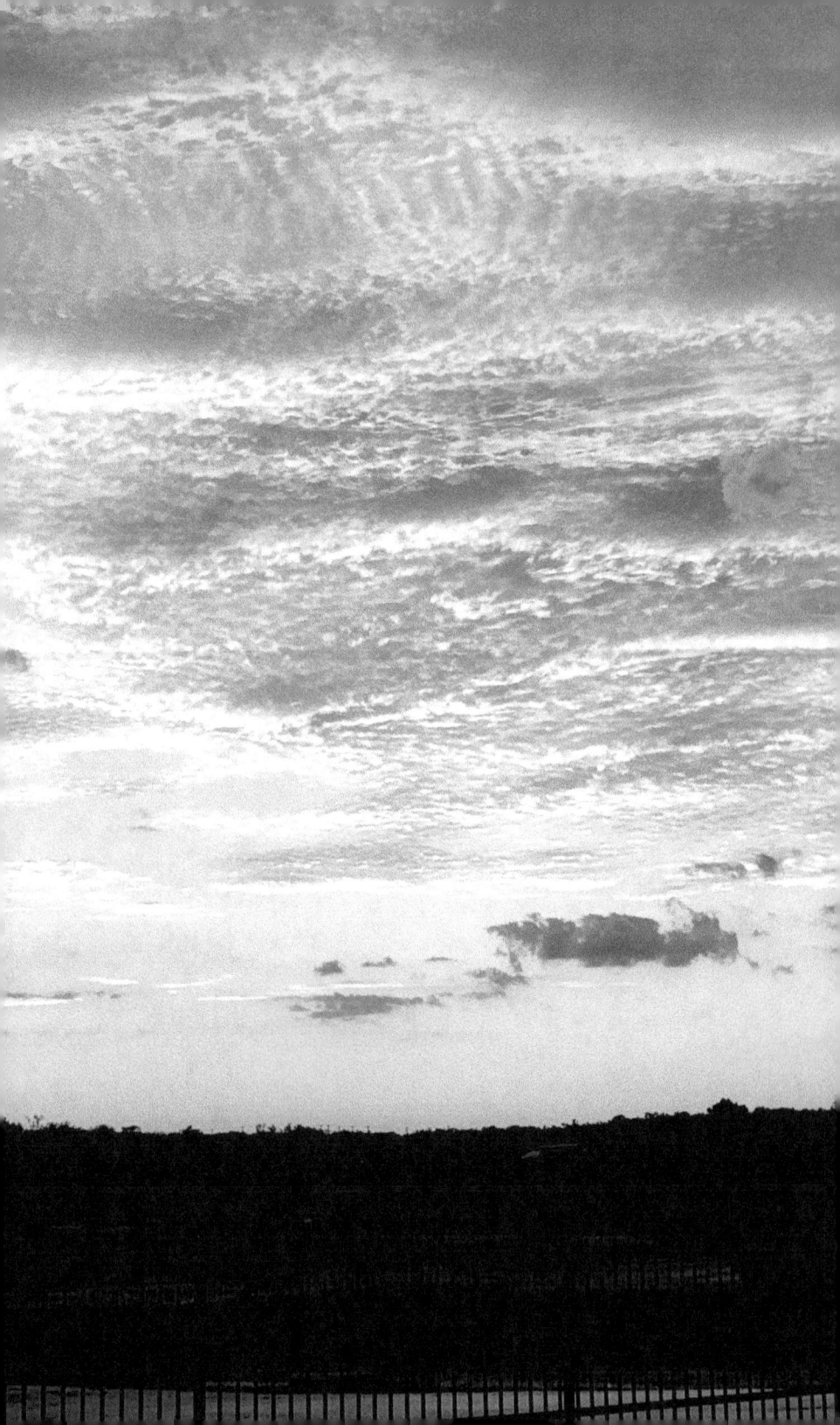

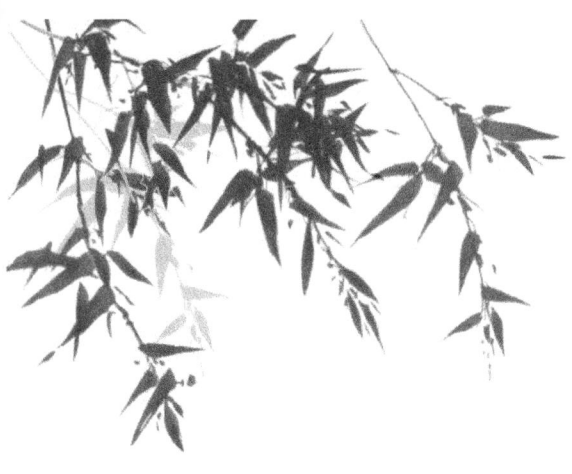

Being able to control fears makes us strong.
Being able to control happiness makes us balanced.

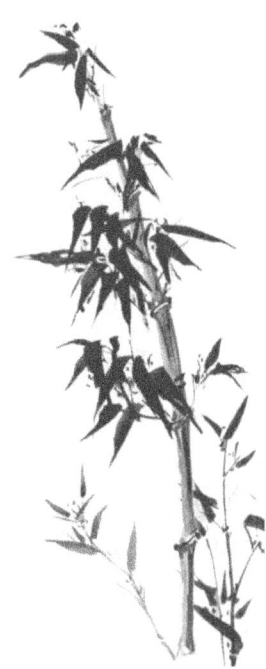

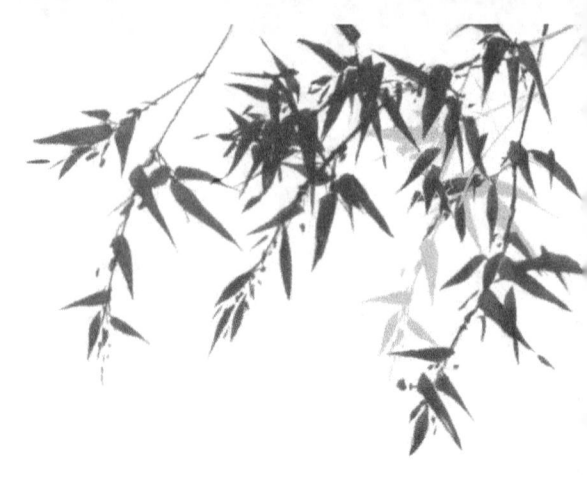

Don't feel that time owes you anything.
Time is steady and continues without failure.
As you should strive to attain.

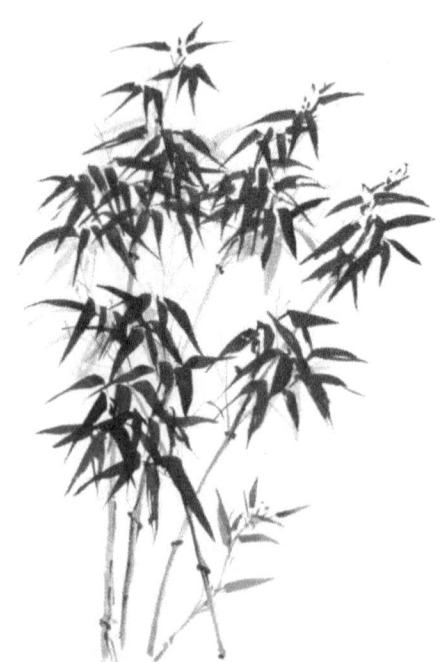

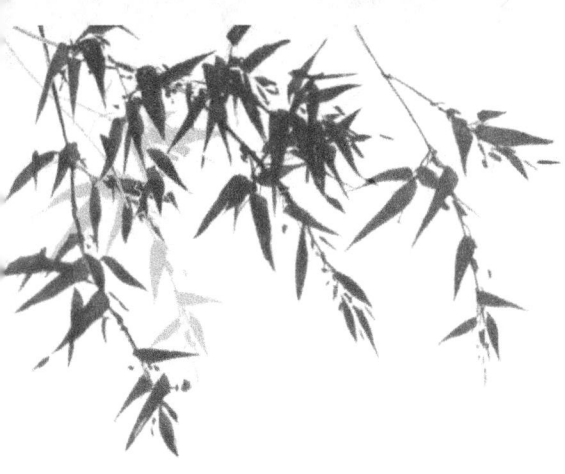

What we think we follow.
Our spirit is our guild to the path of ambitions.

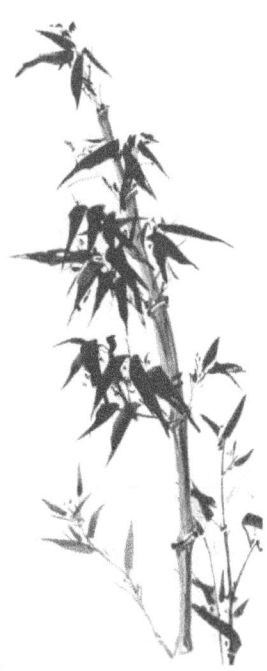

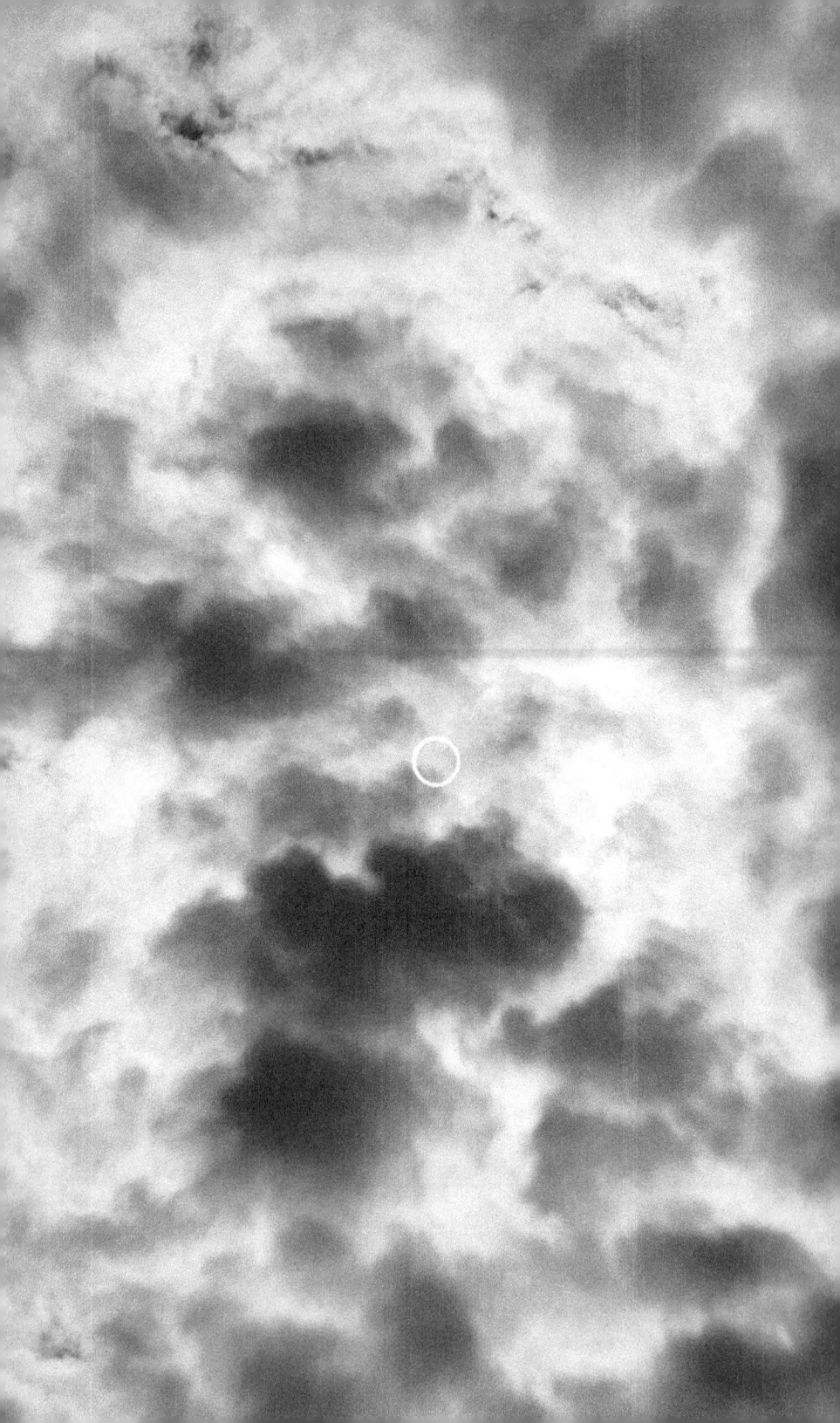

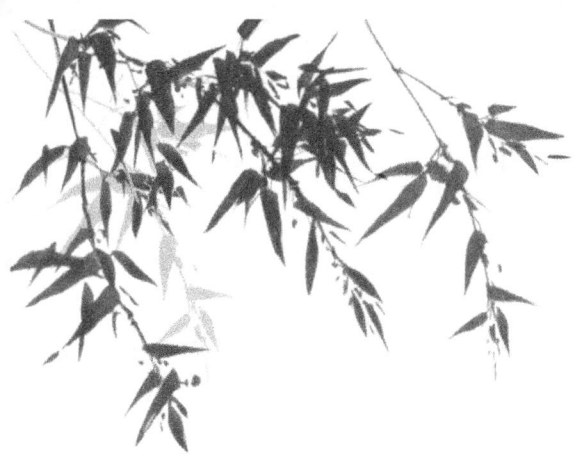

It is easy but it is hard.

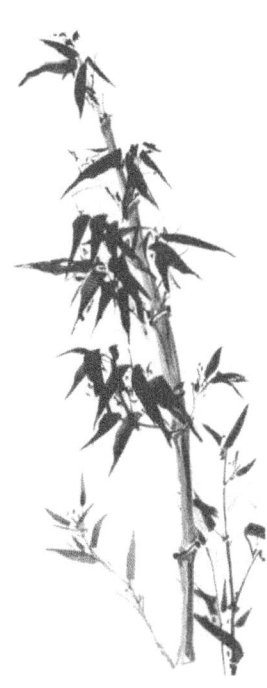

Conclusion

Thank you for reading my book. Many years ago, I started reading and writing eastern and western philosophy. The more I read, the more I felt a passion to write my own thoughts. Once I was enrolled into college studying music, psychology, and any subject I wanted to learn about, I was able to understand creative writing and ways to express myself with pen and paper. These thoughts in this book were written during good (positive) and bad (negative) times in my life.

During my teen years, I had to deal with depression and anxieties. It forced me to drop out of high school and prepare myself for a journey that had many peaks and valleys. A journey that is not for the faint of heart. Everyday was a battle to find balance and become more positive about myself and overcome the tug of war that was inside of me. The more I worked at finding balance by reading and training in martial arts, the more I became able to understand the depths of words, actions, and thoughts.

To find the positive and understand the negative was the key to unlocking the door to the next level of our natural development of life. When I started to understand and find balance in my life, I started to move forward with more success and understanding. I learned life had limitless possibilities and experiences. I started to live for the here and now more and not worry about "what if this" or "what if that" anymore.

Life itself became something I looked forward to experiencing. Later in my life, I started to read my thoughts and realized I had a different outlook on that thought. Life experiences and training had changed my outlook. In turn, I read a thought with new depth and understanding. The thoughts changed for me due to time and change. I hope reading this book can help you understand yourself and life better with time and training.

Remember, we often see the tree but not the roots. The roots are what keep the tree alive and healthy. *Gannbatte Kudasai.*

About the Author

GADIER HEIN GARCIA was born and raised in Texas, USA. Gadier has been studying and teaching martial arts and meditation for over 40 years. Gadier is a 6th degree in the martial arts style of Kenseido, a 4th degree in the art of Kenshindo, and 1st degree in the art of Shorin Kenseikai. He was inducted into the World Pugilist Hall of Fame in 2021.

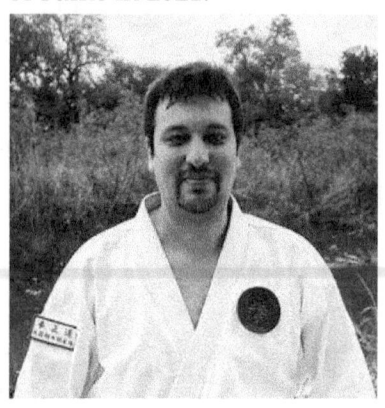

Gadier has helped train kids at a transitional living center with self-empowerment and self-defense classes and has taught women's self-defense classes from a rape crisis center. He graduated from the University of Texas at San Antonio with a degree in Psychology. He worked in the psychological field for 30 years assisting individuals and families. He assisted with the relocation and re-establishment of life for the Hurricane Karina evacuees. He also assisted seniors with re-establishment of life when their apartment complex was destroyed by fire.

Gadier played bass guitar and keyboards for the rock band Winzor. He played cello for four seasons with the Laredo Junior College Civic Symphony Orchestra, performing with musical legends Freddy Fender, Tony Campisi, and Vicki Carr.

Currently he resides in Texas with his loving wife Margaret and their dogs Buster and Toby.